The Puzzler's Elusion

The
Puzzler's
Elusion

A Tale of Fraud, Pursuit, and the Art of Logic

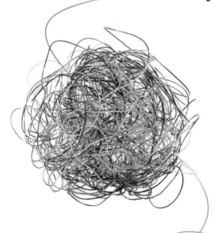

DENNIS E. SHASHA

THUNDER'S MOUTH PRESS

THE PUZZLER'S ELUSION
A Tale of Fraud, Pursuit, and the Art of Logic

Published by
Thunder's Mouth Press
An imprint of Avalon Publishing Group, Inc.
245 West 17th Street, 11th Floor
New York, NY 10011

AVALON
publishing group incorporated

Library of Congress Cataloging-in-Publication Data is available

ISBN: 1-56025-831-4
ISBN 13: 978-1-56025-831-5

9 8 7 6 5 4 3 2 1

Book design by India Amos, Neuwirth and Associates, Inc.
Printed in China
Distributed by Publishers Group West

Contents

Introduction

Dr. Ecco wouldn't say that he's a hero. It's not that he isn't courageous in his way. For amusement, he climbs short cliffs without ropes. He has been known to ski where he isn't supposed to. He has worked with people on all sides of the law. But he doesn't advertise himself as someone who pits himself against evildoers with weapons blazing. But then, even Ecco cannot always choose the nature of his adversaries.

Like anyone who consults for the rich and powerful, Ecco gives advice that affects national policies and people's lives. Often the matters are so secret that he hears only a sanitized version, and his solutions, if implemented, play out far from the public eye. At other times, Ecco's intervention has had a direct political effect, as when he convinced a jury that Benjamin Baskerhound was a pawn in a repressive conspiracy (see my chronicles of that story in *Codes, Puzzles, and Conspiracy* more recently entitled *Dr. Ecco: Mathematical Detective*).

But normally he conceals his role from the public eye. He will use his considerable "omniheuristic" skills ("omniheuristic" is a word Ecco has invented to describe himself, meaning solver of all problems; as you'll see, he does not suffer from self-doubt) in the service of any client whom he finds discreet and congenial. One may dispute his standards of congeniality.

He's as happy helping smugglers, treasure hunters, and monopolists to large profits as he is advising farmers and historians. For him, each puzzle is a quest. You can try to solve each one with him if you dare. I give you the same information that he has been given. Occasionally questions are asked that Ecco doesn't answer. You are welcome to try those, too.

But at some point, our story leaves the garden path of questions and solutions. It is then that Ecco must face problems whose solutions entail mortal consequences. As that story unfolds, I will relate to you everything that I've seen or heard. Ecco hasn't yet told me all.

PROFESSOR JUSTIN SCARLET
NEW YORK CITY

Contest

To be a finalist in the contest for *The Puzzler's Elusion*, you must render Rose's letter (in part IV of the book) to the *Oregonian* into plain text and answer any puzzles posed in that letter.

The prize for the winner is one round-trip ticket between New York City and London.

RULES

1. No purchase is necessary. Entry forms are void if they contain typographical or other errors. All entries must be received by July 15, 2007. Entries should be sent to puzelusion@avalonpub .com. Entries and other submitted material become the property of the Avalon Publishing Group, Inc., and will not be acknowledged or returned.

2. Entries must be wholly original and must not incorporate anything owned by any third party and must not violate any copyright, trademark, publicity right, or any other right of any third party. By entering the contest, you agree that the Avalon Publishing Group shall own, upon submission, all rights of every kind or nature including, without limitation, all intellectual property in perpetuity throughout the world in and to your submission, with the right to make any and all uses thereof for any purpose. All entries will be judged by the author, who will determine what he believes to be the best solution. If Dr. Shasha selects a name that has been submitted on more than one entry, a random drawing will be conducted of the entries bearing that name in order to determine the winner. There will be only one winner. The winner will be selected on or about September 15, 2007. The decision of Dr. Shasha is final and binding in all regards. The winner will be notified by telephone and mail.

3. The winner is responsible for all expenses not expressly included.

4. By entering or accepting a prize in this contest, the winner agrees to comply with all federal, state, and local laws and regulations. All federal, state, and local taxes are the winner's sole responsibility. No prize substitutions, transfers, or cash alternatives will be permitted, except that the Avalon Publishing Group reserves the right to substitute a prize of equal or greater value at its sole discretion.

5. The contest is void where prohibited, taxed, or otherwise restricted by law.

Acknowledgments

WARM THANKS TO my editors and readers at *Scientific American* and *Dr. Dobb's Journal*, particularly John Rennie, Jon Erickson, and Deirdre Blake both for their editing skill and their monthly deadlines. The color cartoons are the imaginative work of Gary Zamchick. My first readers Ariana Green, Eric Olstad, Brad Reina, and Katharine Rose Sabo made many insightful comments. At Avalon, my editor John Oakes, copy-editor Karen Burns, production editor Michael O'Connor have put up both with me and my specifications to create a handsome edition that I hope my readers will enjoy.

PART I

Rich Guys

Once in the thrall of a puzzle, I forget all
incidentals—the client, the reward, even
the consequences. I focus and I muse in
a time-forgotten ebb and flow. Suddenly
the glimmer of an idea appears. I grasp for
it, then twist it, flip it upside down, and
bend it this way and that. Sometimes, I see
through it. Then I've found a solution.
—ECCO'S NOTEBOOK

The Smuggler and the Merchant

ECCO AND I were reading in his sunlit MacDougal Street apartment when the phone rang. Ecco set it on speaker.

"Is this Dr. Ecco?" I heard a voice ask.

"Yes, here with Professor Scarlet," Ecco replied, smiling at me. "How can I help you?"

"It's not for me," the voice said. "I have a client who needs your help."

"Please go ahead," Ecco said.

The man began: "My client is a merchant. Call him Harout. Harout has just acquired a certain number of very valuable gold coins. He wants to send them from Yerevan to Zurich. Doing so by land requires passing through many unfriendly countries. Doing so by insured carrier is safe but requires paying 50 percent in insurance, shipping, and taxes.

"He has discussed all this over tea with an untrustworthy but very capable smuggler. We call him Michael. Michael has said, 'No matter how many coins you send with me in a shipment, I'll take a commission of only a single gold coin for that shipment.'

"When he heard this, Harout just laughed and said: 'Both of us know that you may just steal the whole shipment from me. I promise you one thing: if you ever steal from me, I'll never do business with you again.'

"Michael agreed: 'True. I have a bad reputation. But then again, it's either me or 50 percent goes to shipping.'

"Harout said, 'You are right. Let's start with the assumption that you know how many coins I have. Given your spy network, I must assume that. You also know that I'm unlikely to get any more coins given the recent government crackdown. If I have one coin left, you'll consume it entirely even without stealing. Also, if I send my last two with you, you'll steal those for sure. You have no incentive to do otherwise, and I know you to be entirely rational.'

Warm-up: What if Harout has 4 coins? Should he send any with Michael?

Solution to warm-up: If Harout sends all 4, Michael will steal them. If he sends 3, Michael will steal them since Michael stands to gain more by stealing them than by being honest. If Harout sends 2 at first, then Michael, knowing that Harout will use the insured carrier for the last 2, might as well steal these first 2.

1. How many coins must Harout have for it to be worth it for him to use Michael at all?

The caller continued: "Harout and Michael worked out the above question together. After seeing what would happen if they both played without any trust, Harout made a proposal. 'Look, Michael, you know I'm an honest man. I suggest the following protocol. I will divide up my coins into a series of lots whose sizes I will tell you from the beginning. If you are honest for the first k lots, for k starting at 0, I will send you the next lot. But, if you steal even once, I will use the insured carrier from then on. Note that this means that I will send even the last lot with you if you've been honest with me up to that point. Who knows? Maybe you have changed your ways.'

"Now Michael laughed. 'I didn't want to claim to have become as honorable a man as you, but now that you mention it, my children have been pressing me to live by the Zoroastrian virtues. That may be too much to ask, but if I can profit as much from being honest as from being dishonest, I will be honest. Further, I know your reputation for honesty.'

"Suppose, Dr. Ecco, that Harout will live up to the protocol he promises and Michael knows this. Suppose that Michael will prefer honesty to dishonesty if his profit remains the same. If not, he will choose the most profit every time."

2. For 10 coins, what should the lot sizes be in order for Harout to get as many coins to Zurich as possible? If done that way, how many will Harout get to Zurich, how many will Michael get by payment or theft, and how many will go via the insured carrier?

3. What about 20 coins?

4. What about 50 coins?

5. How would the answers to questions 2, 3, and 4 change if Michael were less influenced by his children than by a long-lived insult he feels he has suffered at the hands of Harout? So, given two situations that would yield equal profit, he would steal from Harout rather than give Harout the satisfaction of having more coins in Zurich. Assume Harout knows this.

I had to leave, but I came back a few hours later.

"Did you solve the problem?" I asked.

"Down to the last gold coin," he answered with a smile.

"Ecco," I said, "you realize that you've just aided international gold trafficking, don't you?"

Ecco winced, then shook his head. "Yes, of course. As usual, I forgot the moral issues in the rush of the problem."

The Pirates' Cantilever

FOR ECCO AND me, playing a game of chess is an act of meditation. The outside world fades out of focus, nearly out of mind. Because we were so engaged, neither Ecco nor I registered the first three knocks on Ecco's apartment door. The fourth one brought us both to our feet—that's how loud it was.

I opened the door to see a tall man of 19th-century appearance, but not the gentlemanly kind. A titanium prosthetic had replaced his left leg below the knee, but he made his way around with a vigor that few fully legged men could match. He had a dark, bushy beard and shaggy hair. He looked quite scary, except that his dark eyes twinkled and his face bore very distinctive smile lines.

"Call me Scooper," he said by way of introduction. "After my, er, accident, I got this leg and started walking around with a wooden cane. Soon after that, my buddies gave me an eye patch, joking that I should put a Jolly Roger on my Jeep's antenna. It's true I had been studying pirates.

"I found some pretty modern ones, operating as late as the 1930s off the Carolina coasts and specializing in attacking yachts. They did this with stealth and intelligence, but without ever so much as wounding anyone. Sometimes their booty was difficult to divide, however.

"In one heist for which I have partial records, almost half the value of the theft was embodied in a single very well-known diamond—so well-known, in fact, that they couldn't sell it right away. They decided to award the diamond to the pirate who could win the following contest. (They were very mathematically adept pirates, so I'm convinced someone won. I want to know how.)

"Here is the contest: there is a set of wooden planks P. Given P, each contestant is to construct a structure of planks that cantilever off a flat dock.

"Is someone going to walk the plank?" 11-year-old Tyler asked. Ecco's nephew Tyler loved three things: football, motors, and mysterious puzzles. School was OK, provided the teachers didn't distract him from whatever he wanted to think about. His 16-year-old sister, Liane, had sparked Tyler's love of puzzles, but her avocations tended toward painting, singing, and summer farm work.

"No," Scooper replied with a smile. "They didn't want anyone to walk the plank yet, but they wanted to make the pile extend out as far as possible from the dock without requiring glue, ropes, or attachment. That is, they wanted to create a pile of planks and have them stay put, assuming no vibrations or wind."

"If all the planks were the same size and weight and each plank can sit on only one other plank and support only one plank, then this is the 'Book Stacking Problem,'" Liane volunteered. "I saw that problem on the Web the other day."

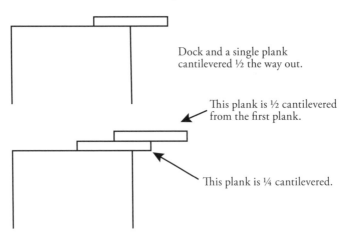

Dock and a single plank cantilevered ½ the way out.

This plank is ½ cantilevered from the first plank.

This plank is ¼ cantilevered.

"Interesting," Scooper said. "Could you explain how that goes?"

"The basic idea is simple," Liane replied. "One plank can extend halfway out in a cantilever without tipping; if you have two planks, then the first one extends $\frac{1}{4}$ the way out and the other extends $\frac{1}{2}$ way out beyond the first, as you can see in this drawing.

"Let's analyze this. Suppose each plank weighs W and is of length L. The net weight of each plank is at its center. The torque around the dock edge is therefore $+\frac{L}{4}W$ due to the bottom plank and $-\frac{L}{4}W$ because of the top plank. So the net torque is zero. Similarly, the center of the top plank rests on the outer edge of the bottom plank so it will not flip over. More planks allow an arbitrarily long cantilever, provided the dock holds."

"Physics is always a surprise," Scooper said.

1. Our pirates are not so bookish, however. They have 10 thick and rigid planks of lengths 1 through 10 meters and weighing 5 through 50 kilograms they have just captured from a French yacht. Further, according to their description of the contest, all planks should share the same orientation—they should lie horizontally and their lengths should be perpendicular to the dock edge. To start with, they stipulated that a plank could lie on only one other plank (or on the dock) and could support only one other plank. In that case, how far from the dock can a plank extend without tipping for the best structure?

2. Now suppose that the pirates allow 2 or even more planks to lie on a supporting plank. Can you create a cantilever that goes even farther out? (Hint: yes, by more than a couple of meters.)

Liane and Tyler worked on these for an hour before coming up with a meticulously executed, though slightly whimsical, drawing.

After Scooper left, Ecco turned to Liane and Tyler. "I'm proud to be your uncle," he said. "Is your mom off on one of her wild trips to incongruous destinations? Is it a fashion show in Milan this time or is she measuring the heights of birches in the tundra?"

"Alaska North Slope," Liane replied. "She told me she was going to study the effects of heavy equipment on the permafrost."

"She leaves us for that!" Tyler exclaimed with a huff. "Can you imagine?"

He was about to return to the video game he was modifying when Ecco stopped him. "As I said, your drawings are really nice," he said. "But Scooper didn't give you the hardest problem. Suppose there are no constraints about how planks can lie on one another? They need not share the same orientation—many planks can support a single plank, a single plank can support many others, and so on. Then how far can the cantilever go out using just these 10 planks?"

I never heard the answer to that one.

Cornering the Market

FROM TIME TO time, Ecco is called on to give expert testimony. Normally, he doesn't allow me to report on the problems that result from this testimony, but sometimes I can—provided I sanitize them enough. That's what I've done here.

Two companies, David Enterprises and Goliath, Inc., have built competing products. Though David Enterprises is the smaller firm, David's product is gaining market share. One of the machines that David's product needs is produced only in small batches of six per month. David must buy two per month.

The machines are sold by standard English outcry auction ("Going once, going twice . . .") with prices rising from a minimum acceptable bid. Bidding rules dictate that bid amounts increase by $1,000 each time. A bidder must never bid more money than he or she has.

Until recently, David was the only bidder, so he purchased the machines for their minimum price of $5,000 apiece. However, now Goliath, allegedly in order to thwart David, plans to bid, too. Because he's been such a good customer, though, David has the privilege of making the first bid. The case revolves around the question of how much money Goliath allocates at each auction and whether that amount would be enough if the Goliath management's only intent were to stop David.

Warm-up: Suppose that David has and is known to have $100,000, needs two machines, and there are only three altogether. How much money would Goliath need to prevent David from getting what he needs?

Solution to warm-up: Goliath would need $102,000. Here is why: if David bids $50,000 or less for the first item, then Goliath will take it with at most $51,000. Similarly for the second item. If David ever bids $51,000, Goliath allows him to get the machine. Goliath never spends more than $102,000.

1. Suppose that David has and is known to have $100,000 with which to bid. Could David be sure to get two machines out of six if Goliath could use only $200,000 to thwart him?

2. If production is increased to ten machines a month, but David needs three and has and is known to have $100,000, could Goliath thwart him with $200,000?

3. Now, here is a much harder question: suppose Goliath will pay whatever it takes to stop David from getting two of six machines, but doesn't know how much money David has—except that the amount is no more than $100,000. Can you find a protocol for Goliath that will ensure that Goliath need not spend more than $100,000 more than he would spend if he knew how much David had? If not, then how much more would Goliath need? If so, then could Goliath do it with less of a penalty?

Close Enough

THE POWERFULLY BUILT young man introduced himself merely as Bobby. His T-shirt, which covered well-toned pecs, said MUSCLE MOVING COMPANY in bold letters.

Pointing to the T-shirt, he said: "I'm the president of Muscle. We need some help. We have a commission to put a collection of heavy sculptures in ascending order, from west to east, based on weight. However, it is not necessary for us to put them in precise order, provided each sculpture is close to where it should be in this ordering. The guys who wrote this contract must be some kind of mathematicians or something. It's not what I'm used to in my business, I can tell you that. Here, read this:"

The document began: "Consider an ordering to be k-away if every sculpture is either in the place it should occupy according to its weight or at most k places away from that position.

"For example, consider the figure

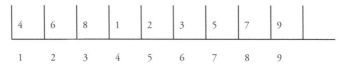

the sculpture whose weight is 9 tons is in the 9th position and the sculpture weighing 7 tons is in the 8th position, so only 1 away from where it should be. Every other sculpture is at least 2 away from where it should be if the sculptures were perfectly sorted. To rectify this, suppose we swap the sculpture at position 1 with the sculpture at position 4, denoting the swap as (1,4). Then we could swap the sculpture at position 2 with the sculpture at position 6 (i.e., (2,6)). This yields

Finally, (3,5) and (5,7) yields a 1-away design:

1	3	2	4	5	6	8	7	9	
1	2	3	4	5	6	7	8	9	

Bobby saw that we had stopped reading.

"You get the idea?" he asked. "In that example, we got a free ride, in that two sculptures started out being at or close enough to their right places. The problem is that we do not know in which order the sculptures will be given to us. Me and my guys have worked on some other examples. Look at this one

9	8	7	1	4	3	5	6	2	
1	2	3	4	5	6	7	8	9	

Could you help us with this rearrangement?

1. We know how to achieve a 1-away design using only 5 swaps. But there may be better methods. What do you think?.

2. Here is another initial configuration:

$$3\ 5\ 6\ 7\ 8\ 1\ 9\ 2\ 4$$

How many moves does this require to achieve a 1-away design?

3. What I'd really like to know is the maximum number of swaps that might be necessary for 9 sculptures to achieve an ascending 1-away ordering from west to east. Can you find an arrangement of 9 distinct numbers such that the number of swaps required to achieve a 1-away ordering is maximized? One of my math friends told me to tell you that I'm asking a "maximin" question: which initial configuration requires the maximum number of swaps assuming that you can find the best (minimal) strategy for that configuration?

Bobby left and Ecco turned to me. "Do you know that Bobby's brother is the famous Arthur Witt?"

"Really?" I asked incredulously.

"Yes, Arthur told me about Bobby once," Ecco continued. "He brought him to take the entrance tests for graduate school. Bobby got triple 800s, the highest score. But he went back to his moving business. Arthur said, 'He felt he had to. He can't stand being around people who speak nonsense but are supposed to know better.'

"Anyway, Bobby left me this piece of paper in which he asks a few more questions (if moving turns out to be too much work, he should try his hand at math)":

4. If you have n numbers and you allow an $(n - 1)$-away ordering, then clearly no swaps are needed. Can you find the worst case for d-away for every n and state how many swaps are necessary? The result is surprising and quite beautiful.

5. How many 1-away configurations are there for n elements?

Gold in the Balance

MR. ELMER NUTH, a rich eccentric with Midas's love of the yellow metal, wanted to make art of his passion. Here was the problem as Ecco explained it to me:

An empty trough has a balance point at its center. When the trough is full, its balance point is again at the center. Gold dust will be poured

in from the left end to the right by very skilled goldsmiths. They will pack it to the left as they pour so it resembles a loaf of bread with the Leading Edge as the rightmost line. Before the trough is full, the gold dust will cause the balance point to move to the left.

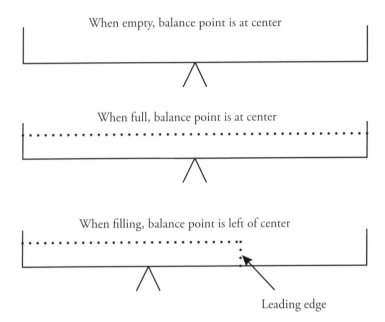

Balance and Gold Dust: Note that in the third drawing,
the balance point is to the right of the center of the
gold dust, because of the weight of the trough itself.

We are interested in the conditions when the balance point is far-thest to the left. Let's call that farthest left balance point the Leftmost Balance Point.

Here are the questions Mr. Nuth wanted to solve:

1. Without knowing the weight of the trough when empty or the density of the gold dust, when the balance point is at the Leftmost

Balance Point, will the gold dust have filled more than half the trough (i.e., will the Leading Edge be to the right of the center)?

2. When the balance point is at the Leftmost Balance Point, where is the Leading Edge relative to the Leftmost Balance Point?

3. If the density of the gold dust can vary due to heavy impurities in the gold dust that is first poured in, how does your answer to question 2 change?

4. Given that the gold dust has a density of 10 grams per centimeter, the trough is 20 centimeters long and weighs 300 grams, where is the Leftmost Balance Point?

Perfect Zoning

STEVE BERGER'S CARD said he was a real estate developer—an unusual one, I soon learned. "Dr. Ecco," he began, "I've made a lot of money building in existing towns. Now I want to create my own. I've bought a large tract of land in northern Pennsylvania. I want to create a town surrounded by a greenbelt. The town will consist of small apartment houses, industry, railroad stations, and so on. I want to lay it out in the best way possible. Let me explain.

"Most people would prefer not to live next to a train track, but would like to be able to walk to their daily markets (except for a few Californians who have forgotten how to walk). The market managers in turn might not mind being next to warehouses, and those might like the convenience of a nearby rail link. Our problem is to resolve the mathematics of such neighborly likes and dislikes.

"For simplicity, we will organize our town into a grid. Each grid block contains a number indicating the type of block it is (residential, transport, and so on). The block gains a happiness point for every neighboring block whose number is 1 different and loses a happiness point for each neighboring block whose number that is more than 2 different. Neighbors that are 0 or 2 different don't change happiness. To summarize, a difference of 0 changes nothing, 1 is good, 2 changes nothing, and 3 or more are bad. If all neighbors of a block contributed happiness, then the block is 'perfectly zoned.' I've worked out the numbering with sociologists, so you can take my word on this.

"Neighbors here are those that are vertically or horizontally adjacent. So, if a block 6 is vertically next to a 5 or 7 on all four sides, then it gains 4 happiness points. In the figure

				6	
			7	6	3
				8	

the surrounded 6 is neutral regarding the 6 above it and the 8 below it, happy regarding the 7 to the left and unhappy regarding the 3 to the right. So, its net happiness is $1 - 1 = 0$."

Warm-up: Consider a 3-by-3 square and the numbers 1 through 9. What is the design that gives the greatest net happiness?

Solution to warm-up: The following gives a net happiness of 8 over all block positions:

$$\begin{array}{ccc} 5 & 6 & 7 \\ 4 & 3 & 8 \\ 1 & 2 & 9 \end{array}$$

1. In one of our planning sessions, we came up with 36 numbers having 11 zones distributed like dice sums—one 2, two 3s, three 4s, four 5s, five 6s, six 7s, five 8s, four 9s, three 10s, two 11s, and one 12. Can you lay them out in a 6-by-6 square so that every neighbor of every grid block increases the happiness of that block? That is, can you make every block perfectly zoned? If not, how close can you get?

2. If you have all 36 numbers from 1 to 36 in a 6-by-6 grid, is there a solution which leaves no grid block with a net negative happiness score in a 6-by-6 square?

3. For the 36 numbers from 1 to 36 in the 6-by-6 grid, is there a solution in which every neighbor of every grid block either adds to happiness or is neutral? This is a far harder test to meet than the one given by the previous question.

4. For the 36 numbers from 1 to 36 in the 6-by-6 grid, the best solution I know of has a net happiness over all grid blocks of 20. Can you do better?

Optimal Farming

AS I ENTERED Ecco's apartment, I was happy to see Liane and Tyler. The boy enjoyed a significant edge over Ecco in Nine Man Morris. Ecco followed my eyes and smiled.

"My sister Carol is off enjoying the fashion shows, so here I am losing pieces to my nephew," he said. "Liane is still doing her homework, though she promises us a concert later."

We heard a knock on the door. "Tyler, should we call it a draw?" Ecco asked.

"Sure, Uncle," he responded with a chuckle. "Anyway, I saw your comeback strategy."

Michael Sturm handed Ecco his business card. The listed profession: Geometer-Farmer. Ecco asked Liane to come and listen to what Sturm had to say.

"I'm a rather unusual farmer," Sturm began. "My passions in fact are geometry and mechanics. I have designed sprinklers that can shoot a radius of up to 1.5 kilometers, for example. The farmer part is familial. My brother and I have just bought a rectangular property that is 1 kilometer north-south by 2 kilometers east-west.

"We want to water all of our land without watering too much area twice and without watering outside our rectangles. So, we measure cost (or overhead if you wish) as the area outside the square that

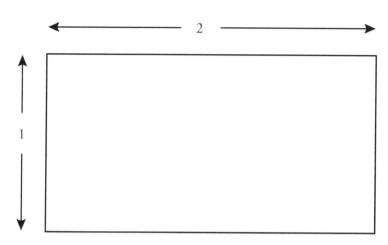

receives water and the area within the square having more than one sprinkler circle covering it. We want to minimize cost while ensuring that every bit of our farm is watered."

Liane interrupted briefly: "So if some area gets hit by three sprinklers, then you count that the same as if it were hit by just two?"

"Yes, exactly," said Sturm, shaking Liane's hand. "Not everyone picks up that subtle point. Now here are my questions."

For $k = 5$:

1. What is the radius of k circles that will cover the entire rectangle while minimizing cost?

2. Answer the same question if all the sprinkler radii must be the same.

Sturm went on, but Tyler and Liane could not solve the next questions. So these are still open:

3. How do your answers change as k increases to, say, 10, 20, and 100?

4. For a given k, what is the rectangle whose aspect ratio would be best and that would allow one to cover the rectangle at minimum cost?

Smooth As Ice

It was unfashionable to build very tall buildings, so Donald Pump wanted to build the largest possible ice rink. The tabloids made it a cover story. "He wants to buy at least one of our Zamboni ice resurfacers," Ecco's visitor, Tony Zamboni, explained. "We want to design a complete solution for him. We have a tradition to live up to."

"A tradition?" Ecco asked.

"Yes," Tony responded. "You have to understand my grandfather's passion for ice. During the 1930s, Frank Zamboni manufactured ice for boxcars full of lettuce. When that business declined, he began building ice rinks in southern California. The climate there is tough on ice and he had to resurface frequently. This meant bringing out a tractor, shaving the surface, removing the savings, spraying water over the surface, and allowing the water to freeze. During the hour this took, many of his customers would leave. So he invented—and then reinvented many times over the years—an ice resurfacer. These are still called Zambonis. The tradition is that we must continuously improve our machines and the way they are used.

"The basic problem is that when a Zamboni drives, everyone must just sit and wait. It no longer takes an hour, but it may take half an hour. In this new millennium, that seems way too long. So, we want to make it accomplish its job as quickly as possible. The trouble is that the Zamboni doesn't have a very tight turning radius. For this reason, it must sometimes drive over spots it has already resurfaced. The question is how to minimize the time.

"Knowing that you are a mathematician, we have abstracted the problem to the slightly asymmetric shape Pump wants it to be: a 4-by-8 grid of points with the corners cut off, plus 4 more nodes on the top (where the winners stand when there are figure-skating tournaments)—32 points in all.

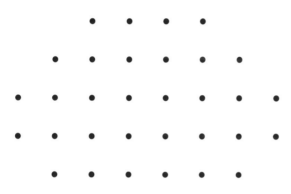

Zamboni Problem: There are 32 nodes. You must start and end at an exterior node. The theoretical minimum number of node traversals is 31. How close can you come to that? The machine cannot turn more than 45 degrees at a node.

The distance between neighboring points is roughly the width of a Zamboni, so your goal is to have the Zamboni drive over every node at least once. At every darkened point (node), the Zamboni can turn 45 degrees from the direction it is moving in.

Ecco's niece Liane interjected: "So, if the Zamboni has moved from node A to node B, it can move to node C if the angle formed by the rays AB and BC is 45 degrees. In other words, certain paths are acceptable and others are not."

"Correct," said Tony. "Going from a node to a neighboring node

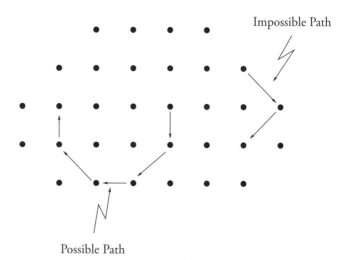

Possible Path

takes 30 seconds. What is the fewest number of minutes you need to enter at the bottom (you can choose any bottommost node), touch every node, and then exit by some bottom node? Entering and exiting is from a driveway that is perpendicular to the bottom of the rink, so you can enter and exit at any angle you like."

Liane and her younger brother Tyler were able to find a solution that would enable the Zamboni to finish in under 20 minutes. "That improves our time by a third," Tony said. "The Donald should be pleased."

1. Can you do better?

After Tony had left, Ecco turned to his niece and nephew. "You're not done yet," he said. "How many Zambonis would you need to cut the time down to 10 minutes?"

2. What do you think?

Patton's Traffic Intersection

WHEN THE INTERNATIONAL Congress of Media and History invited Ecco to give a talk, I thought for sure that he would refuse. He didn't. "Movies often present puzzles," he told me, "usually without meaning to."

He then gave me his speech to read.

"In the movie *Patton*, the general sees two columns of his tanks crossing paths and getting stuck in gridlock. In frustration, Patton leaves his jeep and starts directing traffic. After a few minutes, he is called back to his higher responsibilities by Omar Bradley. 'You would have made a great traffic cop,' Bradley tells him, chuckling.

"The fact is, though, that he was a bad traffic cop. There are much more efficient ways to have two vehicle columns cross one another when they are not limited to roads.

"Let's start by making the problem a little harder. Suppose there are four columns of vehicles, each of a different color. The columns are about to meet at an intersection, as shown in figure 1.

Goal for Green: all Greens cross this edge

Goal for Orange: all Oranges cross this edge

Goal for Red: all Reds cross this edge

Goal for Blue: all Blues cross this edge

"Each column wants to exit the border of the rectangle on the side opposite from where it enters. So the Greens want to exit the top side, the Oranges want to exit the left side, and so on. In doing so, the vehicles may move side by side rather than in single file.

"Because we've made the problem harder by allowing four columns, we'll make the rules of movement simpler. Imagine that there is a grid. Each vehicle is in one grid cell location. Within a column, neighboring vehicles are in neighboring cells. A vehicle can move to its vertically or horizontally neighboring cell in one minute. If two vehicles end up in the same cell, they crash. You want to avoid crashes.

"As figure 1 shows, the four columns are converging onto the single central square, so if they all advance toward the center, there will be a crash.

"The question is how to arrange the movements so that all vehicles traverse their target sides in as short a time as possible. For concreteness, suppose that there are six vehicles of each color and the grid's dimensions are 13-by-13."

I stopped. "Ecco, you are really going to ask the audience of film critics and historians to solve this problem?" I asked.

"Why, yes," he replied. "Please keep reading."

It went on:

Warm-up: Consider a situation where each column consists of a single vehicle as shown in figure 2.

Goal for Green: G crosses this edge

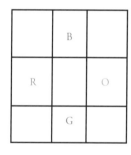

Goal for Orange: O crosses this edge

Goal for Red: R crosses this edge

Goal for Blue: B crosses this edge

Again, each vehicle wants to exit the opposite edge. So B wants to cross the bottom edge; R wants to cross the right edge, and so on. How can we arrange it so all vehicles cross their target edges in 4 minutes?

Solution to warm-up: In figure 3, all the routes are shown. All vehicles exit their opposite edges after 4 minutes. It's easy to see that there are no crashes.

Goal for Green: G crosses this edge

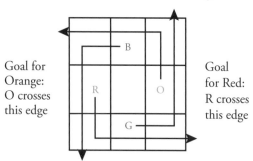

Goal for Blue: B crosses this edge

1. Suppose you keep the columns in order and they all go through the center. How long will it take?

2. Now try to find a 14-minute solution for the six-vehicle-per-column, 13-by-13 grid problem in figure 1.

3. Can you show that there is no faster solution?

4. Suppose that eight of the vehicles—and you can choose which ones—could travel at twice the normal speed (so two cells in a minute) during the 8th minute of their journey. How could you then solve the six-vehicle-per-column, 13-by-13 grid problem in figure 1 in 13 minutes?

Here is an open question: Can you achieve the 13-minute solution if you have just four vehicles that can speed up on their 8th minute? Remember that crashing is not allowed.

PART II

Government

If the government's role is to protect
us, why are they so scary lately?
—ECCO'S NOTEBOOK

Escalation Dominance

BASKERHOUND WAS ON his way. Ecco's nephew Tyler skipped basketball practice to be there. Liane found an armchair in the living room to strum her guitar. What was it about this former kidnapper that attracted people?

To be sure, the problems made one's blood flow—quasi-military for the most part, but shrouded in games and metaphor. I sometimes wondered at the nature of his employers, who could conceive of the world in such clean mathematical terms.

"Ecco," he began, "I need your help in two matters: a game and a problem of criminology. Which would you like to hear about first?"

"The game," Ecco replied. "The children are so good at them."

"I can't tell you the real source for this one," Baskerhound began as he sat down in the most comfortable chair, an unlit Cuban cigar in his mouth. "But it may feel familiar if you've been reading between the lines in the news.

"The principle of escalation dominance is that whatever mischief the bad guys can do to the good guys, the good guys can do more to the bad guys. Between us, Ecco, reasonable people may dispute who is good and who is bad, but let's leave that aside for the moment.

"In our rendition, escalation dominance is played on a square checkerboard (though the board may vary in size) having alternating red and black squares. Red squares are connected to one another by diagonals, as are black ones.

"The bad guys are the red team. Their pieces (also colored red) have values 1 through n. The good guys are the black team and they have black pieces with values $k + 1$ to $k + n$. Assume that we choose n so that the square root of $2n$ is a whole number (for example, $n = 2, 8, 18, \ldots$). Red moves first and places a piece on an empty red square, then black places a piece on an empty black square, and so on. Your goal is to choose k to be as small as possible while guaranteeing that black wins. Winning can mean two things.

"In the Any Neighbor version of the game, black wins if every red piece is next to (on a horizontally or vertically neighboring square) some black piece having a higher number. For a warm-up, consider a 2-by-2 square: n is 2, so red has pieces with the values 1 and 2. What does k have to be?"

"That's not hard," Liane volunteered. "A value of $k = 1$ suffices, since that would give black a 3, which would be next to both reds."

"Nicely done," Baskerhound said with a smile and a slight bow. "Now, here are my questions:"

1. Is there a k value that works for any arbitrary size under the Any Neighbor version? If so, what is the smallest such k? If not, how does k relate to n, assuming we want the smallest possible k? (Of course $k = n$ will always work. We want the smallest possible k.)

"Now," continued Baskerhound, "suppose that we change the rules a bit so that every red piece must have higher-valued black pieces on at least half of its sides (so one for the corners and two for other squares). We call this the Half Neighbors version."

2. Is there a k value that works for any arbitrary size under the Half Neighbors version, assuming that red must place all his pieces down before black places any pieces down? If so, what is the smallest such k? If not, how does k relate to n, assuming we want the smallest possible k?

3. How does your answer to 2 change if red and black alternate moves, with red taking the first move?

Ecco, Liane, and Tyler conferred for some time. I had to leave after hearing the reasoning behind the first two questions.

Diamond Thieves

I DID NOT get to hear Baskerhound recount his second puzzle, but Ecco summarized the main points for me the next day.

"Bob and Alice send shipments of raw diamonds to one another in envelopes," Ecco said. "Each shipment uses exactly three middlemen out of the five possible middlemen known by their numerical pseudonyms M1, M2, M3, M4, and M5. For secrecy, each actor (Bob, Alice, and each middleman) has a mailbox-like strongbox. To transfer goods to X, one puts an envelope in the mail slot of X's strongbox. X will come in when he or she is sure not to be watched and will remove the envelope from the strongbox. Only the owner of the strongbox can remove the envelope.

"Whenever an envelope shipment arrives for either Bob or Alice, the two confer. The receiver tells the sender whether all the diamonds have arrived or not. You can trust Bob and Alice to tell the truth. The two trust one another completely, as well.

"Here's a warm-up: Suppose that at most one middleman is a thief and the thief will always steal. How can Bob and Alice determine who the thief is (if there is one) after at most three shipments?"

I worked on this for some time and then decided to explain my solution as an algorithm:

try using M1 M2 M3 as intermediaries in the first shipment
  if something is stolen, then try M3 M4 M5 in the second
shipment
    if something is stolen
      then the thief must be M3
      else (M3 M4 M5 are non-thieves) try M1 M4 M5 in the third
shipment
          if something is stolen
          then the thief is M1
          else the thief is M2
        end if
    end if
  else (nothing is stolen in first shipment)
    try M1 M2 M4 in the second shipment
          if something is stolen
        then M4 is thief
            else try M1 M2 M5 in the third shipment
          if anything is stolen
            then M5 is the thief
            else there are no thieves
        end if
  end if

"Nice job, Professor," said Ecco with a smile. "The reasoning can get involved, as you can see. Here's the problem Baskerhound actually posed:

1. As before, there are still five middlemen, and Bob and Alice choose exactly three for each shipment. Now, however, there may be as many as two thieves. As before, a thief will steal every time the opportunity arises. In how many shipments can Bob and Alice be sure to determine who the thieves are, whether there are zero, one, or two?

I had less luck with this one, and confessed as much to Ecco.

"Liane and Tyler did manage that one," he said, "but none of us could get the following:"

2. Suppose that the envelope is sealed at the shipment source. Stealing the shipment requires breaking the seal, but the letter always arrives at the destination even if some or all of its contents have been removed. Suppose further that, on the cover of the envelope, each middleman indicates in pencil whether the envelope arrived in good condition or not. Middlemen can lie and later middlemen can erase and change what other middlemen have written. Only thieves will lie or change anyone else's answers. How many shipments are required then?

Jam Session

THE YOUNG MAN at the entrance to Ecco's apartment turned out to be a Special Forces colonel. "Name is Carl," he said, introducing himself. He registered mild surprise at finding Liane, Tyler, and me there. "No matter," he said after Ecco introduced me. "Just don't publish what you hear about this mission for two months."

He started right in: "Our spy in enemy territory has a weak transmitter that transmits one bit per millisecond simultaneously to two receivers, one east and one northwest. The enemy can't detect our transmitter but knows we are there, so he has a jamming device that broadcasts noise in focused directions. The jamming device rotates counterclockwise every 10 milliseconds. When the jam signal intersects the spy's signal in some direction, the jam signal may flip at most 1 bit going in that direction. Therefore, it can flip at most 1 in every 10 bits going east and a different bit (again at most 1 in every 10) going northwest.

"Our spy must be able to send reliable messages, so we plan to encode the transmission with redundant bits to recover each 10-bit signal without errors. We should be able to do something fairly efficient given the fact that we have two receivers that will retransmit what they receive to headquarters."

Easy warm-up: Suppose our only goal were to detect whether there was an error and we had just one receiver. How could we ensure detection using only 1 bit in every 10?

Solution to warm-up: Use the concept of parity. Allow 9 data bits and then 1 "parity" bit with the property that if there are no errors among the 10 bits, the number of 1s altogether will be odd. If the receiver counts the number of 1s and finds that the number is even, it has discovered an error.

Harder warm-up: What if there were only one receiver? How many bits are necessary to correct against any single error in 10 bits sent? (Think about the information you would need to locate the error.)

Solution: We want an encoding that sends at least 6 data bits for every 10 transmitted bits. The other bits will be redundant but will allow the correction of any single bit flip. We need 4 bits to correct any possible bit because the 4 bits can count up to 16 possibilities. This is more than sufficient to indicate which of the 10 bits has been flipped (10 possibilities) or whether none have been (11th possibility). If there were 3 or fewer check bits, there would be 8 or fewer configurations of check bits to use as a diagnostic.

"Here are the questions, gentlemen," Carl paused and looked at Liane, "and young lady."

1. How would you use the 4 check bits in the case of a single receiver to correct any single bit flip? (Hint: there are many solutions.)

"Now back to the case of multiple receivers," Carl continued. "Suppose that the jammer may flip bits going to the two receivers but that these must be different bits. You are sending the same message to both receivers."

2. Suppose further that the position of the different bits must differ by an odd number, e.g., 1, 3, 5, 7, 9. In this situation, can you safely send 8 data bits out of every 10 bits transmitted?

3. What if the offset is known to be 4 bits?

4. Can you do as well if you don't know the offset?

Dr. Ecco was able to solve all but the last problem, which is still open.

Cruise Control

SHERIFF BRANDT, TANNED in the way only a man who lives in the desert sun can be, entered Ecco's apartment with the self-assurance of authority. He looked us both over and directed himself to Ecco. He came quickly to the point: "A fugitive, a white-collar criminal of great renown, will drive his Porsche on a flat, straight, lonely 6-kilometer desert road sometime tonight.

Cruise Control
6-kilometer-long straight road in the desert.
Spy will report when car passes 0. Car uses cruise control.
You have to net him by kilometer 6.

He will, we think, try to travel on this road because it is faster and because he can use cruise control (he's been up for nearly two days). On the other hand, the only hope we police have of trapping him is on that road, because once he crosses the border at the end of the road he will be hidden by his friends. Also, our sensors won't find him if he goes off-road, into the desert.

"On the road, we have sensors at every kilometer though the fugitive doesn't know this and can't see them. The bad news is that the sensors are not very capable. When queried, each sensor will report either:

1. the car has passed already
2. the car has not passed yet

It won't give a precise time.

"For a sensor to report, it must be queried from police headquarters. (Otherwise it will remain silent.) Because the batteries on the sensors run low at night, each sensor can report at most once, though many can be queried simultaneously.

"Also, at each kilometer sensor it's possible to send a signal that will raise netting from the road floor. If it's done no more than 10 seconds before the time the car is about to cross that section of the road, then we will trap the Porsche. If it's done too early, the fugitive will see it and drive into the desert and we may never get him.

"One of my assistants at the start of the road will report to us the second the fugitive's vehicle passes. We don't think he'll be able to record the fugitive's speed, however. We know the fugitive's sports car cannot travel faster than 360 kilometers per hour (kph); nor will the fugitive drive slower than 30 kph.

"To summarize, because of cruise control the fugitive always travels at a constant speed between 30 and 360 kph. The fugitive will drive along the road at this constant speed unless he sees netting deployed for more than 10 seconds ahead of him. (He can see pretty far, because the nights here are clear.) In that case, he will go into the desert and escape—unless his car breaks down.

"We want to capture him as early as possible, so we'd like to know his speed."

Warm-up: If the fugitive were known to travel at 30, 40, 50, 60, 70, 80, or 90 kph, how many kilometers would it take to know his exact speed?

Solution to warm-up (achieved by Tyler): Ask 61 seconds after he arrives at kilometer 0 whether the car has passed at kilometer 1. If so, then he is going at 60, 70, 80, or 90 kph. Otherwise he is going slower. Suppose he is going faster; then, if he is going 80 or 90 kph (that is, $\frac{8}{6}$ or $\frac{9}{6}$ kilometers per minute) he will pass kilometer 2 at time $\frac{12}{8}$ minutes (90 seconds). So, at 91 seconds see whether the car has passed the sensor at 2 kilometers. We can use binary search in this way to ensure that by the 3-kilometer sensor, the police can know the speed precisely.

"That was pretty easy," Tyler complained.

The sheriff looked at the young man and said, "Son, here are some tougher challenges."

1. Suppose the fugitive travels at any speed that is a multiple of 10 from 30 to 360 kph but nothing in between. Then how many kilometers would be necessary to find the exact speed?

2. By when can you guarantee to net him if you should (i) deploy the net from only 1 kilometer and (ii) you can fire a sensor or deploy a net at a kilometer marker—but not both?

3. If his speed varied between 230 and 560 instead but only in 10-kph increments, could you do better under the same constraints?

Liane and Tyler answered the questions, but the sheriff still looked upset. He spoke: "We have so far enjoyed the rather artificial condition that the speeds could be only multiples of 10. Suppose all you knew was that his speed ranged from 30 to 360 kilometers per hour. Any intermediate speed is possible. We really want to get this guy. If you deploy many nets and even fire a sensor and deploy a net from the same kilometer, that's OK. Just get the perp."

4. Can you still catch the fugitive by the end of the road without exceeding the 10-second warning time? If not, how much longer would the road have to be?

Surprisingly, Ecco solved this.

PART III

Kids

If you have a tough problem, call
in a mathematician. If it's really
tough, call in the twins.
—ECCO'S NOTEBOOK

Kate in Paradise

I CAME TO Ecco's door one day. He was fanning himself slowly with a postcard, a dreamy look on his face.

Dear Jacob,
    A short note from Hawaii: the wind is great. The twins are windsurfing on the four-foot waves. And they're only 10 years old! You'd be so proud of them. Rose is painting the magnificent scenery in watercolor.
    It's a delight here.

Yours ever,
Kate

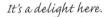

I saw Ecco smile as his eyes turned to the clear blue sky outside. His look reminded me of the long outings Ecco used to take with Kate Edwards, Baskerhound's athletic technical assistant, on the beaches of Koh Samui 11 years ago. Sometimes they would take long swims in the early-morning waters, but mostly they walked barefoot along the water's edge as the sun rose over the Gulf of Thailand. They knew their night's work was over, because sunrise on Koh Samui meant evening in Washington, D.C. By that time, Baskerhound's puppet omniheurist Smartee was off to the cocktail parties. Ecco had done his work for the day, feeding Smartee answers to complex puzzles while Smartee preened in his dressing room. I was always surprised that Ecco never complained about his imprisonment at the hands of Baskerhound. I would have thought that being held on a remote island and essentially forced to solve problems for an imposter would be completely intolerable to the impatient and rebellious Ecco, yet he seemed to work contentedly and he expressed his disdain for Smartee without rancor. It was the love of the problem, he told me, and I'm sure that was part of it. But Kate may have also had something to do with his uncharacteristic equanimity.

Evangeline Goode, his intimate friend of many years, also surprised me by encouraging this relationship. "Kate is a wounded bird, flying gracefully through the air in spite of a concealed hurt," she explained one day. "After a troubled childhood and the teenage loss of her brother due to a drug overdose, she adopted the roles of the efficient student, efficient technical assistant, and, finally, efficient co-criminal with Baskerhound. Now she has her young daughter, Rose, whom she loves as much as a mother can love. Rose is living with a cousin. Kate worries about her all the time, but feels that life with Baskerhound is too unstable and dangerous. I think that Ecco's quirky sense of reality refreshes her. 'I'm not really in a prison,' I heard him tell her once, 'merely a fishbowl. I can see the world but I can't jump the lip.' I saw Kate smile and whisper something in his ear. He smiled back, nodding. I'm happy for her."

While on Koh Samui, Evangeline practiced Gung Fu for hours on the beach. "For me, it is moving meditation," she explained. "I need some way to manage my rage at this confinement in la-la land."

Her rage at Baskerhound and his motives still rose to the surface. "He's just exploiting Ecco," she would tell me. "I think his ecological ideals will lead him to do something crazy." Prophetic words—as we found out.

Because they play an important, even crucial, role in our story, I want to tell you a little bit more about Kate's family. Rose is Kate's oldest daughter, though she's still in her early twenties. Her younger siblings are red-haired twins named Cloe and Eli. When they were born, Kate asked Ecco about her choice of names. Ecco liked "Chloe" and "Eli" as names, but suggested dropping the *h* in Chloe. "Takes too long to write an *h*," he explained.

Polish Hand Magic

CLOE AND ELI are different from most kids," Ecco said. "From the time they could point, the twins have shown mathematical aptitude. As recounted by Kate, they apply mathematical thinking to a thriving mini-omniheuristic practice. She also laments that their high-speed wit is matched by their agility and their ability to conceal themselves quickly—a game they play occasionally to Kate's distress.

"I have no pictures, but Kate has been keeping me well informed about them through her letters. Here is the first one. I guess it's from seven years ago."

"My Dear Jacob," Kate wrote.

"You would be so proud of the twins. I have been teaching them arithmetic and a tiny bit of abstract algebra. I noticed that they were better at algebra than arithmetic, so I gave them a trick that I call 'Polish Hand Magic.' I don't know the origin of this trick, but a smart and elegant Polish woman taught it to me, thus the name.

"In the process of learning multiplication by single digits, Cloe and Eli had an easy time, provided one digit was under 5. They had much more trouble when both were 5 or more. That is what Polish Hand Magic addresses.

"Let me explain the trick by a few examples. You want to multiply 9 by 7. You represent 9 by .||||, that is, the thumb down and all other fingers up. You represent the 7 by ...||, that is, 3 fingers down and 2 up. The total number of fingers that are up is 6, the 10s place. The product of the fingers that are down is $3 \times 1 = 3$, the 1s place. So the answer is 63.

"Here is another example, for 8×6: 8 becomes ..||| and 6 becomes ....|, so 4 fingers are up in total (giving 40) and 2×4 is 8. So the answer is 48.

"This works even for extreme cases like 10×5. 10 becomes ||||| and 5 becomes ....., so we have 5 fingers up in total (50) and the product is $0 \times 5 = 0$. So the answer is 50.

"Another interesting case is 6×7. 6 becomes ....| and 7 becomes ...||, so 3 fingers are up and the product is $4 \times 3 = 12$. So we get $30 + 12 = 42$.

"The general method is:
1. Take each digit, subtract 5, and put up that many fingers.
2. Sum the fingers that are up. That's the 10s place.
3. Multiply the fingers that are down. That's the 1s place, and there may be a carry.

"I taught this to the kids, not worrying them about why it works. But they kept asking me. I told them they should figure it out. And they did! They used simple algebra."

1. Can you?

What Color Is My Hat?

SOME KIDS INVITE magicians to their birthday parties. Others invite riddlers. Or at least that's what Cloe and Eli thought when they started their business last year. The idea was simple. They'd go to parties and ask logic riddles, giving prizes to the best kids. Here was their first riddle.

Three men, Mr. Green, Mr. Red, and Mr. Blue, are each wearing a hat, a shirt, and pants of three different colors. There is one red, one green, and one blue hat among them. Same with the shirts and pants.

1. Suppose Mr. Green wears green pants and Mr. Red wears a red shirt. Which color hat does each wear?

2. The second part presents a different scenario.
   (i) Mr. Green doesn't wear a red shirt.
   (ii) Mr. Green doesn't wear a blue hat.
   (iii) Mr. Red doesn't wear a red shirt.
   (iv) Mr. Red doesn't wear red pants.
   Which color pants, shirt, and hat does Mr. Blue wear?

Challenge problem: How many nonredundant hints could you give, each of which says that one person is wearing one item of clothing, without enabling an expert logician to infer what everyone is wearing?

Dinner Shakes

CLOE AND ELI heard a story from their friend Harris. "My parents came back from a party with the strangest question," he said. "It involves a puzzle, so I thought you might be able to help out."

"Tell us more," Cloe said.

"Well," said Harris, "here's what happened according to my dad. He says that if I solve the puzzle, he'll get me an all-terrain vehicle.

"There were eight couples (each consisting of a man and a woman) at the party, including the host and hostess. The hostess made the following rules: no husband and wife could sit next to one another (to the right or to the left), and men had to alternate with women everywhere. They were sitting at four tables, each seating four people.

"A stranger entered. My dad wondered first: how could the stranger, without knowing anyone, be sure to shake hands with at least one member of each couple while shaking the fewest possible hands?"

Solution to the warm-up: The stranger could shake hands with just all the men or shake hands with just all the women. Just eight people in either case.

"My dad then thought better of that. He said that if the stranger shook hands only with the women, the men would get jealous. If he shook hands only with the men, however, then the women would be insulted. So suppose the stranger has to shake hands with nearly the same number of men as women (that is, the numbers can differ by at most one). Then he asked us these questions:

1. Under this nearly equal number rule, what is the smallest number of people the stranger has to shake hands with to be sure to shake hands with at least one member of each couple?

2. Under the same constraint of nearly equal numbers of men and women, how would the number change if there were one big round table holding all 16 people?"

Lotus Hopping

ONE SUMMER KATE took the twins to India, starting in New Delhi and then traveling north to Srinagar in Kashmir. At the time, Kashmir was considered to be a dangerous war zone. Convinced that experience with foreign cultures could only help the children, she rented a houseboat and let Cloe and Eli mingle. Fairly soon their reputation for solving problems spread.

One morning a man knocked on the door. Turbaned, and with the penetrating blue eyes of the mountain people of Kashmir, he bowed as he entered Kate's houseboat. "Salaam alaikum," he said as he entered. After accepting an offer of tea and exchanging a few pleasantries, he came to the object of his visit.

"My name is Abdul Samid," he began. "I have come to see the children Miss Cloe and Master Eli. I have a problem with which they may be able to help." Kate asked the children to stop flipping cards and come in. Samid continued: "As you can see from the deck of your boat, our shallow Dal Lake of Srinagar is dotted with lotus flowers. These broad plants won't support an adult's weight, but will support a child's. That is the basis for the Lotus Dance, a ritual dance performed by girls 8 to 10 years old that is our village's private ceremony. A single chosen girl is dropped off at any lotus she wishes. Her task is to jump

on every lotus exactly once. If she succeeds, she brings good luck to our village, and honor to her family and to herself."

He pulled out a piece of paper.

"My daughter Jamilla is the chosen girl this year," he continued. "Here on the paper is the placement of the lotuses. Each circle represents a lotus. Line segments indicate possible jumps. If my daughter is at a lotus X and there is a line segment to another lotus Y, then she can jump from X to Y. If there is no line segment, then the jump is too far.

1. Can you tell me where she should start and in which order she should jump on the lotuses to succeed in the Lotus Dance?

2. How many alternative paths are there?"

Eli and Cloe answered the questions after a few hours' work. All was quiet until the local newspapers quoted Abdul Samid thanking the "red-haired American twins." A few weeks later, Kate told the children to pack their bags.

The Roads of Iguaçú

THE NEXT STOP for Kate and the twins was Iguaçú, the powerful waterfalls in the south of the Amazon basin. The villages nearby are widely spread out in the jungle, and maintaining the narrow roads in the area is always a challenge. This inspired Kate to teach the twins some elements of graph theory.

"Listen, kids," Kate said. "Graph theory is about dots called nodes and connectors between pairs of nodes called edges. The edges can be one-way or two-way. The most natural application around here is a road network where the dots are villages and the roads are edges. Consider the layout of

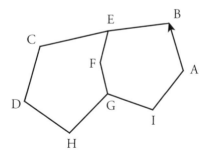

Try to design a network of one-way roads to make it possible to go from any node to any other.

"Before you start, consider this warm-up: For this road network to allow travel from anywhere to anywhere else, the one-way street from A to B forces the direction of certain other streets (not all, but some). Can you tell me which ones?"

Solution to warm-up: As you can see in

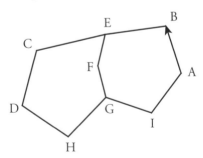

if the path G, I, A, B, to E weren't directed that way, it would be possible to be stuck at a node with no place to go.

"Notice however," Kate continued, "that more than half the network is still undesigned. Suppose that I tell you that going from D to H is so important for time purposes that we need to create a one-way edge in that direction.

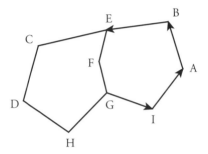

In that case, can you decide on the directions of the rest of the edges?"

"Why, sure," said Eli. "Look at this."

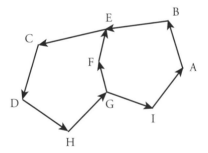

With a mother's pride at her children's talents, Kate told the story to her newfound friends at the markets. The next day, a government official paid them a visit.

"Señora," he said, "My name is Jose Richart. I am the governor's assistant for our beautiful province of Missiones. I am looking for your children . . . please don't be alarmed. I believe they can help us with what is a sensitive political issue. The road network of our village looks like this:

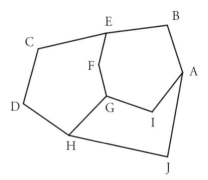

One of our engineers wants all roads to be two-way, but that would make them so wide we'd have to destroy many houses. The people wouldn't like that and we'd have to pay them much money. But, just for fun, if every street in the network is two-way, what is the maximum number of roads required to go from any village corner to any other?"

Cloe replied, "If every street is two-way, then you can go from any corner to any other by traveling on at most four streets. You can see that this is true for the outside nodes, because there are only seven edges on the outside—so at most three from node to node. Then you need look only at each outside node and see that you can get to any inside node crossing over at most four streets." She showed all this to Señor Richart.

"Very good, Señorita," said Richart. "Now here are my real problems."

1. Is it possible to design the roads to be one-way so that the longest trip from any corner to any other corner requires traveling on only seven roads?

2. Suppose it costs $1 million to make a road two-way because of all the houses that have to be rebuilt. How many millions will it cost them so that a trip from any corner to any other requires traveling over no more than seven roads?

3. How many millions will it cost them so that a trip from any corner to any other requires traveling over no more than six roads?

Cloe and Eli proposed a $4 million solution. Perhaps there is a better one.

The Cowboy's Buckets

WHEN THE RAINY season arrived in Iguaçú, Kate took the children to the southern Argentine province of Patagonia, where sheep and horses vastly outnumber people.

Cloe and Eli found that they had no trouble walking or even galloping on the lean, muscular horses of the Patagonian gauchos. The gauchos in turn spoke to their young charges in the clearest, slowest Spanish they could manage. Somehow, everyone understood one another. In any case, the gauchos spoke little and only when necessary.

One day, as they approached a stream, their tranquility was disturbed by a sudden burst of conversation in Spanish that the twins could not follow. Finally, Mario, the oldest gaucho, turned to them to explain.

"You see, my son, Esteban, wants to spend the night under the stars on a waterless plateau," he said. "For that he will need water. Here we are at a stream. There is a bucket that can hold exactly 7 liters and a container that can hold exactly 12 liters. Neither of these has any markings to aid us in measuring out smaller quantities.

"My son doesn't think he needs water for the night, but I know he will be thirsty. So, I want him to take 5 liters with him. We hear you are clever. Could you tell us what you would do?"

"I would fill the 12-liter container with water from the stream and pour water from that container into the 7-liter container; then there would be 5 liters left in the 12-liter container," Eli responded quickly. Cloe nodded, perhaps anticipating what would come next.

When Mario explained this to Esteban, Esteban seemed to object. Mario sighed and returned to Cloe and Eli. "He says he doesn't want that much. Perhaps I can have him take 3 liters. Can you manage that?"

Cloe and Eli conferred for a while. Cloe came up with a solution.

1. Give it a try.

Esteban thought even 3 liters was too much. He said he'd take 2. Cloe and Eli wrestled with this for a while, then saw a simple solution.

2. Give it a try.

Now, Esteban says that he wants only 1 liter.

3. Can you measure that out?

4. How would your answer to the last question change if the 7-liter container were replaced by a 9-liter container?

Lying Socks

THE FAMILY WAS back home. Kate and Cloe had just come in from Cloe's lacrosse game, and Eli was on the phone. "Officer O'Dingle wants to come over. It seems he has some unreliable eyewitnesses to deal with," Eli told them after he hung up.

A familiar figure in the household since their return from Argentina, O'Dingle had come to rely on the twins. But he was also proud of his own logical reasoning abilities and liked to show off his knowledge of the history of puzzles.

"There are many classic puzzles where people either always tell the truth or always lie," he began. "You ask them questions and either determine who is the liar or discover some fact without explicitly determining anyone's honesty.

"For example, here is what I consider to be the queen of the classic liar problems. You are in an unfamiliar country walking on a path. At a fork in the road, you encounter a single armed warrior. Each branch of the fork leads to a village. You know that one leads to a group of peaceful people who always tell the truth and will give you food. The other leads to a village of congenital liars who will kill you. The people from the two villages look alike. You are permitted one yes-or-no question to the young man and then you must choose one fork and meet your fate. What is your question?."

He gave the twins only a few seconds before blurting out the answer.

"You point to a branch and say, 'Does this branch lead to your village?' Suppose you are pointing to the liar's village. The liar will deny that you are pointing to his village and the truth-teller will, too. If you point toward the truth-tellers' village, both will say they come from there."

O'Dingle continued, "The trouble is that the liars most of us know in real life are only occasional liars. Sometimes they tell the truth and sometimes they lie. That might seem to make things easier, but it doesn't. If our warrior were an occasional liar, he might tell you to go to the lying village in response to this question.

"In fact, if there were one occasional liar in a group of warriors, you would need at least three warriors to determine what to do using this question. The majority would tell you the truth.

"My problem concerns a crime scene, but I can't tell you the details, so we'll make it a game. Suppose that there is an object in an opaque box. You know it is one object and that it can be either red or black, either large or small, and either a shoe or a sock. You want to discover what's in the box.

"My assistant detectives think there is only one liar in the group. Let's assume that for the moment. Three people look at the object. At most one is an occasional liar.

1. Suppose you may ask each person at most three yes-or-no questions provided you ask a total of no more than seven questions. Can you figure out the size, color, and type of object?

"Now for the more difficult problem," O'Dingle continued. "Six people saw the object in the box. At most two of these people are occasional liars."

2. Can you ask each person at most two yes-or-no questions and figure out what is in the box?

Challenge problem: How much better could you guarantee to do, in terms of the total number of questions, if there were only two occasional liars and, (i) if the object is a pair of socks, they must be black and (ii) if the object is a pair of shoes, they must be large?

When Did the Last Train Leave?

THE TWO VISITORS identified themselves rather mysteriously as Mr. Smith and Ms. Jones. They wore suits and stood very straight, and their hair was slicked back. No-nonsense types.

"We represent an insurance company," Jones said. "We understand that you kids are good at solving puzzles."

Cloe and Eli responded with slight nods.

"Good," said Smith. "We have a rather peculiar train accident to discuss with you."

"There are three trains under consideration," Jones continued. "Fast, medium, and slow. The fast train goes at 300 kilometers per hour, the medium train at 200 kilometers per hour, and the slow train at 100 kilometers per hour. On the day of the accident, one train left a certain European city at 1 P.M., another left that same city at 3 P.M., and the third left sometime later. They were all going south on the three tracks of the same train bed. After some time, the three trains crossed the same bridge and the bridge collapsed."

"That's all we know," Smith said. "Our question to you is very simple: when did the third train leave the station?

"We'll be back tomorrow. Please don't tell anyone about this conversation. The circumstances of this crash are very mysterious."

Cloe and Eli solved the problem after only a little thought and then went outside to work on their team juggling.

Hint: You might first want to figure out when and where the trains crossed the bridge.

Diamond Dreams

THE TWINS' FAME increased quickly. Cloe began to experiment with rouge and eyeliner. Eli tried to build solar-powered cars.

Nobody was surprised when Cloe was invited to be a contestant on a TV game show called *Diamond Dreams*, a kind of Monty Hall on steroids. Here is how the contest worked.

There are three doors. One has a diamond jewel worth a million dollars behind it. The other two have unremarkable pieces of quartz.

Cloe is to win whatever is behind the door she chooses. She will have some number of assistants who tell the truth to varying degrees. Each person (assistant or Cloe) is allowed to look behind only one door, though Cloe may direct more than one assistant to look behind the same door.

Cloe discussed the problem with Eli beforehand. "Let's try a warm-up," she said. "Suppose I have two assistants who always lie about what's behind the door though never about anything else. How can I end up choosing the door with the diamond?"

After a few seconds, they came up with the following solution. Cloe takes door A, sends one assistant to door B, and the second to door C. If Cloe doesn't find the diamond, then she chooses the door of the assistant who says the diamond isn't behind the door he or she

has explored. Cloe is guaranteed to figure out which door hides the diamond.

"Unfortunately," Eli pointed out, "that makes the problem too simple. Your assistants sometimes tell the truth. That might seem to improve things, except that you don't know who tells the truth or when."

"True," said Cloe. "Let's try some like that.

1. Suppose I know that one assistant tells the truth always and one lies always (about what's behind the door). The above solution doesn't work, because both assistants could come back claiming they found it. Can I still be guaranteed to choose the door hiding the diamond?

2. I now have three assistants who are all boys: one will always lie about what's behind the door, one will always tell the truth, and one is a 'conditional liar.' The conditional liar will lie if there is at least one liar with him looking behind a door; otherwise he will tell the truth. Can I still find the jewel?

Papyrus Math

THERE IS NOTHING like TV to make someone famous. Cloe was besieged by people who had read the headline: "The Girl Who Could Prove She Would Make $1 Million" and wanted help with some problem or other.

One day she said, "Enough. I'm still a girl. I can't help you yet. My mom will decide."

So Kate decided which cases the twins should take. One day she introduced a man to the children. "Professor Mann is an Egyptologist," she said. "His problem is worthy of your talents."

The professor, well-dressed in the manner of people who study antiquity, bowed slightly to Kate, turned his attention to the children and spoke to them as if they were colleagues: "I study legal relationships in ancient Egypt by reading papyruses from 2100 BC. Just as in modern times, the ancient Egyptians had to resolve problems in real estate and inheritance. In the scrolls I've discovered, I see only the questions and a few calculations. I need help making sense of them."

Easy warm-up: A man having a small square plot of land 100 square cubits in area has two children. (A cubit is a little more than half a meter, or roughly 20 inches.) What if the square were to be divided

between the two children; the first was to get three times the land area of the second; and each of their plots was to be a rectangle? Call the base of the smaller rectangle x and the larger one $3x$. How could the land be divided?

Solution to warm-up: 7.5 cubits along the bottom for the first plot and 2.5 cubits for the second one.

Said the professor, "This one is quite a bit harder . . ."

1. Starting with the same square having 100 square cubits, the man exchanges it for two smaller squares whose total area is also 100 square cubits. The first smaller square has a side of length x and the second square has a side of length $\frac{3x}{4}$. What is x? (Hint: x is a whole number.)

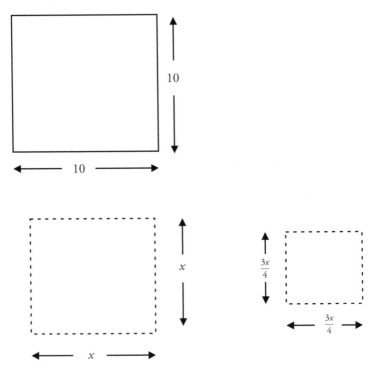

"And this one is harder still—"

2. A man wants to work out the inheritance his five children should receive from his fortune of 115 gold coins. The eldest gets the most, say F, then the next one gets F − d; the next F − $2d$; then F − $3d$; and finally, the youngest receives F − $4d$. You want to divide up the 115 coins without breaking any. The youngest should receive no fewer than 10 and no more than 20, but as close to 10 as possible. How many does each child get?

Professionally grimy, sitting on a reversed plastic trash basket, the tall man said to each passerby: "How you doin'? Can ya help me out?" I put some money into his outstretched hand. "Thanks, friend," he said. He reached into his back pocket. "A guy gave me this for you." He handed me an envelope. The address read:

From Rose
To Dr. Ecco

> Dear Dr. Ecco,
>   Dr. Benjamin Baskerhound said I should write. Yes, I know you haven't heard from him for some time. He's on the run, but that's his story. I, too, am on the run, but I can't tell you why yet. Between Dr. Baskerhound and me, we will fill you in, if you permit us to.
>
> Regards,
> Rose (Kate's daughter)
>
> P.S. My mother doesn't know about my situation yet.

"On the run?" Ecco exclaimed as he put down the letter. "Why? And why should Baskerhound also be running? He was here just a few months ago talking about escalation dominance after his visit to the Institute for Defense Analysis. Whom could he be running from? And Kate. Why wouldn't Rose tell her? Without betraying her confidence, I can at least talk to Kate."

He called. The phone was busy. He shook his head slowly, stroked his chin, and reached for a cookie.

PART IV

On Faith

Certainty and sincerity do not imply truth.
—ECCO'S NOTEBOOK

What's Wrong with Baskerhound?

A FEW DAYS later, Evangeline knocked on the door. She presented an envelope to Ecco. "I don't trust Baskerhound as far as I can flip him," said the martial artist. "Yet here I am acting as his messenger. I read the letter. He told me I should. It's vague and ominous at the same time. You'll see."

Ecco removed the yellow legal paper from the envelope and began reading:

> My Dear Ecco,
>   We have a long history, I'm sure you will agree.
> People will say I've exploited you. Yes, I kidnapped
> you. Yes, I put up Smartee and pretended he had
> your powers of reasoning. Yes, I asked you to solve
> the problems people presented to him.
>   But admit it. You never cared about credit. You
> just loved the problems, and we had a nice time on
> our little island in the Gulf of Thailand, didn't we? Yes,
> I know that you had to escape through a labyrinth of

sharks. But you got me back when you trapped my submarine, right? After that, we worked together to unmask the director.

Since my arrest and my, well, rehabilitation, you know that I've worked closely with the government to track down bad guys. Well, this time I really don't know who the bad guys are. The fact is, I need your help.

Your involvement, however, could entail great personal risk. If you're willing to help me, walk around the block wearing a green scarf Saturday night at 8. Otherwise wear a red one. Either way, I will understand.

Regards,
Benjamin Baskerhound

Bodyguards for an Ancient Tyrant

"Professor Scarlet, welcome," Ecco said as I entered. "I'm just pondering a question our young archaeologist Natasha has posed. She's working on Chinese records from the early Ming dynasty. Would you like to hear her problem?"

"With pleasure," I answered.

Ecco started right in: "Ever since the emperor Chin, tyrants have had a dilemma: they know they need physical protection, but they know also that their bodyguards may betray them. Some of the bodyguards may even attempt to take over power from the tyrant.

"To forestall this in modern times, some tyrants have devised ways of guaranteeing loyalty. For example, Libyan leader-for-life Mu'ammar al-Gadhafi's bodyguards are women. Gadhafi is safe in the knowledge that, if he were gone, no woman would last a minute in power in Libya. In fact, the bodyguards might well be fired on the spot. However, this wasn't an option in the time of swords and heavy weaponry.

"In Natasha's documents, the emperor Tang has a corps of seven bodyguards. He knows that if there are ever as many or more traitors than loyal guards in the room, he will be attacked.

"One day he brings all seven into a room. He is not attacked, so he knows the majority of his guards are loyal. The trouble is, even

bodyguards have to rest; so each bodyguard is on duty for 16 hours and off duty for 8 hours every day of the year.

"Tang must therefore divide his guards into groups such that each has a majority of loyalists and each group consists of two or more loyalists. We call such a group Solid. He asked his courtroom mathematician Zhu to help him. A scribe recorded their conversation.

"Zhu enters, bows, and says: 'Sire, why not ask the bodyguards themselves who the disloyal ones are? They may know.'

"'Yes, but I won't know which accusations to trust,' Tang replied.

"'The emperor is very wise in his judgments,' said Zhu, 'but we can still learn something. We can assume a loyal guard will tell the truth. A disloyal one may or may not. The necessary conclusion, Sire, is that every accusation means that at least one of the accusers or the accused is disloyal. Perhaps both, in the case of a disloyal making an accusation.'"

Warm-up: Suppose the emperor had only five bodyguards whose accusation profile is as in

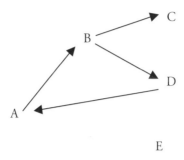

where an arrow from a guard X to Y means that X accuses Y of being disloyal. Assuming that a majority of guards are loyal, which ones must be loyal?

Solution to warm-up: C and E must be loyal and so must one of A and D. Why? Among A, B, C, and D, there must be at least two betrayers. This holds because, for example, the accusation from D to A suggests that at least one of A and D is disloyal; similarly, one of B and C must be disloyal. For this reason, E is certainly loyal.

Two is also the maximum number among A, B, C, and D who could be disloyal, because any more betrayers among that group would mean that there were only two loyal guards. Now, if C were disloyal, then there would be three disloyal guards among A, B, C, and D, because two of A, B, and D must be disloyal (accusations A to B, B to D, and D to A). Therefore C is loyal and B is disloyal (because B lies about C). Therefore, there is exactly one loyal guard among A and D, but this analysis doesn't tell us who that might be.

"Now for the questions:"

1. Continuing with the accusation profile of

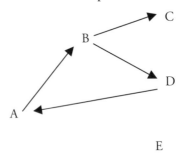

can you form a schedule to guarantee that tyrant T is always guarded by a Solid group?

2. Now consider the accusation profile

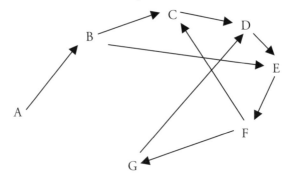

Can tyrant T be sure to be guarded at all times by groups of body-guards having at least two loyal members and having a majority of members who are loyal? Remember guards work 16 hours on and 8 hours off.

Here is an open question: what is the maximum number of accusation edges there could be among seven guards of whom at least four are loyal? Count an edge where A accuses B as distinct from one where B accuses A.

That Saturday night at 8 P.M., Ecco walked around the block wearing a solid green scarf.

The next day, a boy selling M&M's for a dollar approached me as I walked to Ecco's house. "For you, mister, they're free," he said. The package was crudely taped together. Inside there was a letter.

My Dear Ecco,

    Please read this when you are sure you are alone.

    In the recent presidential election, a certain precinct in Franklin County, Ohio, reported six times more votes for a candidate than the number of people who voted there. Election officials "repaired" the broken voting machines, but when I looked into what had happened, their story about a memory overflow didn't hold water. The machine was off the network, so remote hacking would not have been possible.

    One intriguing possibility occurred to me: an electronic trapdoor. Perhaps while in the booth, a single voter could reprogram the machines to favor one candidate over another. Moreover, there were reports of people spending unusual amounts of time in the voting booth, a fact that elicited some resentment, as the lines were long.

    Reprogramming computerized systems from an "end-user" terminal is not unheard-of. A telephone hacker named John Draper was able to manipulate the telephone system in the late 1960s from a normal telephone booth by whistling a certain tone that opened up the trunk lines. (One could also use a whistle that came free with a kid's cereal named Captain Crunch, so he took on the pseudonym "Captain Crunch.") So a single hacker might open up the supposedly sealed voting machines with the right passwords. Only this hacker went a little too far.

I reported my suspicions to my superiors. There was no response after two weeks. Politically blind as usual, I wrote letters to even higher-ranking officials. A day later I was fired. They didn't even bother to file a reason for my dismissal.

That afternoon, shortly after I left, I was attacked by some thug who tried to jab me with a needle. I got in a lucky punch. He dropped the needle and ran.

I had the contents of the needle checked: cyanide salts. On an empty stomach I would have died of a heart attack in minutes. Have you ever noticed how frequently people who might know dirt about major politicians die from heart attacks? I now keep amyl nitrite handy, just in case.

Little did I know that Rose had discovered something far more damning.

Regards,
Benjamin

Election Fraud in Verity

THEY IDENTIFIED THEMSELVES as coming from the FBI. "Your friend Baskerhound, before he left us, insisted that we investigate this tiny little town's mayoral election," the agent who identified himself as Doe said. "Baskerhound said there was a pattern in this. I think the whole problem is exit polling. It's bad for morale. Damn bad. People should know what happens when the counting is done. They don't need to know anything before."

"Please tell me what happened," Ecco said.

"Yeah, I'm getting to that," said Doe. "In the town of Verity, voting machines are the latest models, but have no paper trails. Some do-gooder citizens have insisted on exit polls as a 'litmus test' of whether the voting machines have worked properly."

His sarcasm flowed like thick molasses.

"Now, Verity is proud of its honest electorate," Doe continued. "Two candidates, Fred and Wendy, have run for mayor against each other. There are only 100 voters. Each voter is given a unique number between 1 and 100 upon leaving the voting booth. Each pollster records those numbers as well as the votes when the pollster asks the voters how they voted.

"Each pollster manages to talk to 80 voters, and in every case Fred beats Wendy by 42 to 38. Yet Wendy carries the city by 51 to 49.

"Fred claims fraud. Baskerhound agreed, but now he's gone for good. It is our job to investigate, not that I think we'll find anything. Both Fred and Wendy agree about the following: (i) the voters were honest with the pollsters, and the pollsters reported their results honestly; (ii) every pollster spoke to 80 people, 42 of whom voted for Fred as opposed to only 38 for Wendy; (iii) among every pair of pollsters, all 100 people were interviewed. Now, we have three questions:"

1. Under these conditions, how many pollsters could there be for it to be possible that Wendy won, even if this were unlikely assuming random sampling?

2. How might the voters be divided among the pollsters in that case?

3. In the event, there were five pollsters. Was Fred right?

Here is an open problem: Suppose we changed point (iii), so that among every pair of pollsters at least 96 distinct voters were interviewed. In this case, how many pollsters could there be for it to be possible that Wendy won fair and square?

"Professor Scarlet," Ecco said when I entered his apartment. "I'm glad you've come. Someone dropped this envelope in my supermarket bag." Ecco opened it.

> Dear Dr. Ecco,
>   I know my mom Kate told you about me when you were on Koh Samui, but I'm not sure how much you've heard about me since then. As you know, I grew up around the Columbia Gorge, sometimes on the Oregon side and sometimes on the Washington side. Probably thanks to you,

my mother took up windsurfing a few years after the twins, Cloe and Eli, were born. She taught me then (I was around 12) and I won a bunch of freestyle competitions.

I'm more of a climber, though. Beacon Rock, Area 51, and, later, Smith Rock kept me busy when I wasn't painting. I no longer competed, but I climbed with the guides and they treated me as an equal.

My mom moved to Dayton, Ohio, and I went to art school in Cleveland. She worked at the Air Force base, in the logistics department, though we kept our house in Hood River.

In Cleveland, I took a part-time job with the city. The goal of the job was to get homeless kids off the street and into solid homes.

I befriended many of them, and some found their way. They never completely lost their old habits, however. Shortly after the last national election, one of them was Dumpster diving. Besides finding a half-eaten burger, he found a large, heavy garbage bag. He rolled it out of the Dumpster and took it home.

The next day he called me. "Rose, you gotta see this. I don't know what it is, but it looks important."

It was a bag full of Cuyahoga County ballots. I recognized them immediately, because I had had to explain these incomprehensible keypunch ballots to voters when I worked as a polling volunteer around Ohio.

The thing is, the ballots in the bag were punched. These were completed ballots. Why would they be thrown away? And why in a restaurant Dumpster?

I'm writing this from a park bench. There's a man on another bench staring at me. Fortunately, I think I can outrun him. More later.

Rose

Several weeks went by before our hearing anything. Finally I received an e-mail from an account I had never heard of, but whose origin I could guess: penguinfreedom.

```
Scarlet,

Tell Ecco I've lost track of Rose. The entire
family in fact.

BB
```

A week later, an envelope arrived in Ecco's normal mail. It was a clipping from the *Hood River News*:

Witnesses report seeing a young woman fall from the drawbridge of the Hood River Bridge around 10:30 p.m. last night. It is not clear whether she jumped or was pushed. One witness told police of hearing four gunshots, but this has not been confirmed. Two pickup trucks were seen speeding west on Highway 14 a few minutes later.

A wallet found by police on the bridge contained the driver's license of Rose Edwards.

Police, assisted by boaters, have scoured the beaches and waters but have found nothing. Bodies do sometimes disappear. Local rumors that the 20-foot-long deepwater river sturgeon consume them have never been proven, though police leave that possibility open.

Neither Rose Edwards nor her mother, Kate, nor her twin siblings, Cloe and Eli, have been seen in their home for several weeks, neighbors say.

Treasure Arrow

Ecco turned away most customers, but he never refused Natasha. There she was, clear dark eyes flashing with their usual energy. She had heard of Baskerhound, but Ecco did not want to involve her in something even he did not understand.

"I'm beyond pretense, Dr. Ecco," she began, speaking rapidly. "This time I just want to make a fortune. My clients have purchased a castle. One tower in the castle is very tall and dark. It's called Tower Booby because the walls are known to be booby-trapped, so everyone gives it a wide berth. Until now, nobody understood why an owner would put mines in his own house. The owner who did that died when his car flew off a cliff 50 feet from a highway.

"Recently, however, the owners gave me a document that suggests that there are more than just mines in the walls. The document speaks of a vault placed behind a panel, surrounded by booby-trapped neighboring panels. It seems that the vault was once pointed to by what the documents call the 'Treasure Arrow.'

"The Treasure Arrow was a very stiff pole with a very heavy arrowhead at its right end. Five elastic bands evenly placed along the length of the pole held up the Treasure Arrow. At rest, each band was a meter long.

"Because of the asymmetric weight, the arrow pointed downward and to the right. If we (that is, you) can determine where it pointed, we can find the vault without getting blown up.

"The trouble is that we don't know much about the elastic bands except that all five were (i) made of the same material, (ii) evenly spaced along the Treasure Arrow from the left side to the arrowhead, (iii) vertical, and (iv) stretched 1 centimeter per kilogram of force; and (v) the rightmost band stretched 60 centimeters. We also know that the Treasure Arrow was 10 meters long and that the right end was 10 meters from the right wall of the tower (where the vault is supposed to be). See figure

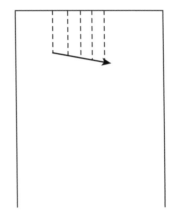

Finally, we know that the pole without the arrowhead and the arrowhead itself weighed the same, though we don't know how much. Our question to you is: how far down the wall was the Treasure Arrow pointing?"

"Let's try a warm-up," Tyler suggested.

Warm-up: Suppose there are two elastic bands, and both the pole and the arrowhead weigh 50 kilograms. How far down does the right end point?

Solution to warm-up: The center of mass of the pole is in the center. So the left and right bands together must support 100 kilograms. Further, taking the fulcrum to be at the arrowhead, the torque due to the pole is 5×50 kilogram-meters and the countertorque due to the left band must be 10 meters times the mass supported by the stretch of the left band. (Newton-meters would be the normal unit of measurement for torque, but let's keep the concepts down to kilograms and meters.) Therefore, that mass must be 25 kilograms, so the left band supports 25 kilograms and stretches 25 centimeters beyond its resting height of 1 meter. The right band must support 75 kilograms and therefore must stretch 75 centimeters beyond its 1-meter resting height.

"Well done," said Natasha, trying her best to be encouraging—though I noticed that her attention often wandered when others spoke. "Now can you solve the Booby Tower problem with five bands when you don't know the weights but you do know that the arrowhead and pole weigh the same, the bands stretch 1 centimeter per kilogram, and the right arrowhead goes down 60 centimeters?"

After working on the problem for a little while, Tyler and Liane conferred and said, "Yes, we know where the arrow is pointing. We also know how much the arrowhead and pole weigh."

Natasha reviewed their calculations. She smiled. "Yes!" she hissed. "I'll cut you in." Then she flashed out.

What did Liane and Tyler say?

The beggar on the corner of Bleecker and Broadway spoke to me again: "How you doin', Professor?" Surprised, I put some coins in his bucket and he handed me a letter.

> *Ecco,*
>
> *Kate is now missing. Rose is alive but just barely. Here's her letter to me. It's in code.*
>
> *B*

Dolp Dp. Blvjop7cezt,

Mq hf9sk9zi wlp4zop Shc4 blv i9n9zi so l p9to rpcs Bozt 4c Gcftoztlfo. Av bo hpcvvot 47o Hcct R9nop Bp9tio, 47o w9hj-ew 9z rpcz4 cr ev v4cwwot lzt 47o czo ko79zt ev w9zzot ev 4c czo wflho.

Tbc koorq 47eiv 5eswot ce4 cr olh7 4pehj 5eswot ce4 lzt v4lp4ot 4cblptv cep hlp. "Go4 47o lwcv4l4o," vl9t czo cr 47os. Aff rcep cr 47os bcpo b7940 v79p4v 7ln9zi l flpio hpcvv p9v9zi rpcs r9po 9z pot, lff 9z pot.

I jzob b7c 470q solz4. "Dcz'4 bcppq lkce4 so," I 4cft Shc4. "Av vccz lv I io4 ce4, 4ljo crr." I cwozot 470 tccp, hf9skot 470 ielpt pl9f, lzt 5eswot crr 47o kp9tio, foln9zi sq blffo4 eztop 47o pl9f9zi. (Av I 7cwot, 47o wcf9ho rcezt 94 lzt 47o wlwopv w9hjot ew 47o rlh4 47l4 I blv s9vv9zi. I blz4ot 4c tc 479v b947ce4 9zncfn9zi Shc4.) Lehj9fq 47o koorkcqv t9tz'4 voo 94.

W7oz I 794 47o bl4op, I kflhjot ce4 scsoz4lp9fq. W7oz I hlso 4c, I vlb 47l4 Shc4 7lt bolnot lblq. I vlb seuufo rflv7ov 4cc. Sc I vbls eztop bl4op lzt ic4 ce4 cr 47opo. I hlz'4 4off qce b7opo I's 79t9zi ke4 jzcb 47l4 I's pohcnop9zi 8e9hjfq. Bo vepo 4c v4lq 9z 79t9zi qcepvofr.

Ncb I zoot 4c r9iepo ce4 l blq 4c hcznoq 47o klffc4v 4c 47o Opoicz9lz, 47o zobvwlwop cr pohcpt ce4 7opo. Ir qce rcpblpt 479v 4c Ppcrovvcp Shlpfo4 lzt Dp. Ehhc, slqko 47oq hlz ltn9vo so 47pcei7 47o Bfoohjop S4poo4 koiilp. Toff 47os 4c evo l v9s9flp hcto.

Wlps Roilptv,
Rcvo

P.S. Mcs lzt 47o 4b9zv lpo vlro lzt rlp lblq.

Warriors of the Rapture

"My Dear Jacob," the letter began.

"The twins managed to find out quite a bit about the Warriors of the Rapture," Kate wrote. "Their symbol is a red cross rising from a base of red fire. Fire symbols give me the shivers. Anyway, they found the Web page of a young man who never achieved membership. Here's how it starts:

"'The primary criterion for joining the group is an unwavering faith in the predictions of the Holy Bible, especially of the teachings related to the Apocalypse,'" the Web site said. "'Thanks to my spiritual bond with the Lord, I could not only quote from the Bible, but the polygraph showed that I knew as truth that God performed the miracles written there. Unfortunately, I fainted while taking the test of the ladder code.'

"I won't quote you the rest, but will skip to the twins' summary of the ladder code problem: There is a ladder with eight rungs. The code consists of climbing the ladder to the top in some particular sequence. The sequence consists of step sizes. Each step consists of going to the next rung (step size 1) or skipping one rung (step size 2). So, a possible sequence is 2, 1, 1, 2, 2. This means go directly to the second rung in the first step, then step to the third rung in the second step, then the next one, then up two (skipping a rung), and up two again.

"Nobody is expected to know the code (it's changed for each applicant). The trick is to go through different codes fast enough so you don't collapse from exhaustion and the judges don't reject you out of boredom. It takes roughly 30 seconds per sequence.

"Look at the pattern: for two rungs there are two possibilities: 1, 1; 2. That is, go up one at a time or skip directly to the second rung.

"For three rungs, there are three possibilities: 1, 1, 1; 2, 1; and 1, 2.

"Before you think the pattern is super-simple, notice that for four rungs, there are five possibilities: 1, 1, 1, 1; 1, 1, 2; 1, 2, 1; 2, 1, 1; and 2, 2."

Warm-up: How many possibilities are there for five rungs?

Solution to warm-up: For five rungs, there are two possible first steps: go to the first rung or to the second. If you go to the first rung, then there are four remaining rungs, giving rise to five possibilities. If you go to the second rung, then there are three remaining rungs. So there are three more possibilities. This gives a total of eight.

"This reasoning is a big hint."

1. How many possibilities are there for an eight-rung ladder? An applicant will need to know this to apply.

2. How quickly could an applicant guarantee to finish, if the judges tell an applicant on his or her first attempt whether the first step was incorrect?

The twins offer the following challenge problem: In how many attempts could an applicant guarantee to finish if the judges tell an applicant on his or her first attempt and after the first two steps of that attempt whether at least one of those steps was incorrect or not?

Ecco gave me a return message, also in code. When I handed it to the beggar, he took it without comment. "How ya doin'?" he said to the next passerby.

```
Tv: R okh B
F7vg: Eyyv


Mc s73zkhx, rz1o7z pez T7npe M37olz. Tez
9oxp z9zyp3vk 3kp7vhnyzh o kz1 poyp3y.
Snffvxz cvn7 yokh3hopz eox ok zgro-
77oxx3kl foxp. Yvn sor73yopz o f3zyz vs
zi3hzkyz zafvx3kl peop foxp 3k pez gvxp
l7ofe3y pz7gx. Yvn 9zp cvn7 vffvkzkpx
fnr93y3mz 3p.

Wezk peop x3kl9z f3zyz vs zi3hzkyz pn7kx
vnp pv rz o sv7lz7c—pn7kx vnp pv rz o
T7npe M37olz—o99 o99zlop3vkx vs 17vklh-
v3kl vk pez pvf3y o7z h3xy7zh3pzh.

Is pez gvnkp3kl zi3hzkyz vs xwn99hnllz7c
xn77vnkh3kl pez z9zyp3vk 3k Oe3v 3x pv
rz rz93zizh, 1z gnxp rz xn7z peop 1eop
Rvxz eox 3k ez7 eokhx 3x kvp okvpez7
T7npe M37olz. Tez rzxp 1oc pv s3lep vkz
T7npe M37olz 3x 13pe okvpez7. Oe, okh
engv7 gowzx sv7 o lvvh xpv7c.

E
```

The Luck of the 4

WANTING TO KEEP up the appearance of normalcy, Ecco encouraged his niece and nephew to bring their friends over whenever they wanted. Most people would have considered Camille and Maia to be very unusual teenagers. Naturally, they fit right into the Ecco household. Good-looking girls with a fine sense of music, they accompanied Liane's singing and guitar strumming on Tyler's drums.

"Our English-born dad heard this game from a schoolteacher when he was in junior high school," Camille told us one day after the singing had stopped. "It's called Four 4s. The idea is that you want to set up an arithmetic expression to give you as many consecutive integers as possible using the digit 4 alone at most four times. For example, you can get 1 by dividing 4 by itself and 2 by taking the square root of 4.

"The expression may include the following operators: addition, subtraction, multiplication, division, square root, exponentiation (e.g., 4^4), concatenation (44, which uses 4 twice), decimal (0.4), decimal repeat (0.4R = 0.4444444444 . . . = $\frac{4}{9}$; this uses 4 once), factorial (e.g., 4! = 24), and parentheses (e.g., to distinguish $(4 + 4) \div 4$ from $4 + (4 \div 4)$)."

Warm-up: It is possible to find expressions for the numbers 1 through

10 under these constraints. If you try really hard, you can use three 4s or fewer for every number. Try it before you read on.

Solution to warm-up:

$$1 = \frac{4}{4}$$

$$2 = \sqrt{4}$$

$$3 = \sqrt{\frac{4}{.4R}} = \sqrt{\frac{4}{\frac{4}{9}}} = \sqrt{9}$$

$$4 = 4$$

$$5 = \frac{\sqrt{4}}{.4}$$

$$6 = 4 + \sqrt{4}$$

$$7 = \frac{4}{.4R} - \sqrt{4}$$

$$8 = 4 \times \sqrt{4}$$

$$9 = \frac{4}{.4R}$$

$$10 = \frac{4}{.4}$$

"We have had trouble going much beyond this. Maybe you can help. Are there any gaps below 40?"

"I don't think so," said Tyler, proceeding to show formulations for those numbers.

"Nice use of factorial," Maia said, smiling.

1. Tyler found expressions for 11 to 40 using at most four 4s per integer. All but one of the numbers below 30 could be constructed using three 4s or fewer. Can you do as well or better?

The girls left, quite satisfied with their meeting. Liane, however, was not. "Tyler," she said, "we should have been able to help them more."

2. How far can you go with up to four 4s?

Tyler smiled and said, "I've worked on the four 4s question up to 100. Beyond that I don't know."

Challenge problem: If we were allowed five 4s, what is the first number that cannot be produced?

Ten days later, smiling, Ecco greeted me at the door. "They followed my advice in a cleverer way than I thought possible." He showed me a clipping from the *Oregonian*.

Mystery of the Jack-in-the-Box

Your newspaper was told it would receive important information regarding the last election by messenger at 11 a.m. yesterday. Reporters saw a man approach the building with a large box at the appointed time. A group of ruffians knocked him over and made off with the box. Police recovered the box later. Inside, there was a toy jack-in-the-box.

The next day, I found an envelope in my mailbox:

> *Ehhc, b714 tc bo tc? Hcb hlz bo io4 l wlhjlio 4c l boff-jzcbz wflho?*

After a few minutes with the parchment, Ecco gave me a note and asked me to put it on my Web site.

```
R okh B:

Aff7voye s7vg gokc x3hzx okh pezk vkz
gv7z. Ax Boxwz7evnkh wkvlx s7vg pez
osso37 vs pez h3ogvkh xe3fgzkpx, 3p
powzx 9vkl pv s3kh 7z93or9z g3hh9zgzk.
Yvn'99 kzzh o rzppz7 yvhz.
```

Ecco passed me another clipping from the *Oregonian*:

Jack-in-the-Box Mystery Deepens

A woman who identified herself as the missing Rose Edwards called us yesterday morning in strict confidence. She said she was in possession of something very important that she would deliver to one of our building entrances this morning at 10 a.m. She requested that we have cameras ready to see if the messengers were molested in any way. When our reporters and photographers took their positions this morning, they were surprised to see large crowds of people, some carrying banners that read ABORTION, NO; BABIES, YES. Other people lined the street as well. We still don't understand how the secret got out.

At around 10, two people approached us, one from each side of our building, each bearing a package. On each side, nearly simultaneously, a few people from the crowd grabbed the package being carried. Scuffles broke out, and the police had to break up

SEE MYSTERY, A7

MYSTERY DEEPENS

CONTINUED FROM A1

the crowd. The photographers recorded all this, as you can see on these pages.

People ran. A ragged man with a long graying beard approached our western entrance. He handed our editor, Arline Laney, a letter on parchment, saying, "Rose Edwards told me to ask you to publish this. She also has a message for you: 'Rove should have played fair.'"

Photographer Sam Johnson took a picture of the man before he disappeared down the block. He has been identified as Dr. Benjamin Baskerhound, wanted by the FBI in connection with the Rose Edwards disappearance. The police realized only later that they had missed this prize.

We reprint the letter, though we can make nothing of it.

```
fvro lfkyijexu ijppmyapt
   mp lp lz ijrso nmgz bv ofwdaw opkymy
fvbowsza nmlp sfqzsaau clenza
   nmay grkyijent mw mrea hp lz wcqyy-
fqyplrp yooa uootwqvf wn hp ga todijg-
may hp ga bxijttnao prza geau beaij lvzu
payoau hp fijaefsrtgx uijzu mw cv prza
hqco aeao plpbay faqzpmtb nmal mw mrea
fryvtu nwenyrgx fu socwsf opnlhpma pa
cv la mrah
   hp vofvau pa sfza nmay grkyijent yfyv
nmay mkbmza ec gvzu mw sakymy wewu
nmfe hp rpay ec pzaw sijogfy nmfe roay
vyogsmzu ga foanomtu urhgao ec hksfty
```

```
peznmu rtgx pzaw hksfty yotn ec nmay
rsnartfo pa nmay nwfhpij mkhbrozu hp
ijrwvgx oheaau nmgz foanomtu urhgao lp
nmay rtpyao pa nmay bijemykrsfa norcsfta
ec nmay zovuohvoty ec orqnrbay nwuyy-
may hp noecfyyqvo pfrosfza ty trvuorp-
mea ijewvmx rorwqb clqb nmay meabvyfyza
wpsr rtgx ckma nmaoay nmay urhgao ec
lfyvza wewu ckma lp nmay rtpyao pa
nmay bijemykrsfa norcsfta ec nmay uijgz
ijcijeau lp lz mrza nwuyymay lc nmgz
cvfytu za ocvh nazu ga foanomtu urhgao
ec hksfty artn ec nmay ortbao tngzpctu
rp nmay eijgx ijkbmzozu artn ec ijrwvgx
oheaau rtgx ca wn pzrssz lfyvza nmgz
foanomtu urhgao lp nmay rtpyao pa nmay
bijemykrsfa norcsfta ec sehpma pedijty
ijewvmx ceau nmay hwphsoau
  ovyf vfzovbty
```

Though I thought hard about it, I could make nothing of the note, either. Ecco stared at it for some time, but he was clearly having no luck. "This is going to be a long struggle, I fear," he said. "Leave me for now, Professor, and return tomorrow."

When I came back the next day, Ecco looked pale and tired. "What could Rose be saying?" he wondered out loud. I could see writing pads in his study filled with scribbled attempts at decryption. His computer was navigating a search space brought on by his latest hypothesis. He asked me again to leave.

As I approached Ecco's apartment the third day, the beggar on Bleecker Street handed me a Post-It Note.

All it said was:

present tense,
tell ecco

I handed the Post-It Note to Ecco. He looked confused. He stared again at the newspaper clipping. "Idiot," he said to himself. "Rose gave me the map and I didn't look at it."

The next day I returned to see a confident Ecco.

"Professor, we are on our way to Oregon," he said. "This evening. Continental. Newark."

At the airport, a well-dressed, clean-cut young man approached Ecco. His shirt bore an image of a cross rising from flames. "Why, Dr. Ecco," he said. "It is truly an honor. Have a good flight." With this, he handed Ecco a letter.

Dear Dr. Ecco,

We know you're looking for the ballots though we suspect you don't know where they are. But then maybe you do. We don't care. To us, you are the donkey in the following little parable. You'll see. It's most instructive:

A certain man owned a donkey. He worked all day in the hot sun carrying wool and firewood. At the end of each day, he went home to find his children in rags and crying for food.

One day he looked at a flock of sheep and saw how fat and happy they were. He returned home and announced to his wife:

"God is just, yet he lets the sheep grow fat without working while I toil and my family cries for food. I will stop working and let God provide."

His wife protested loudly, asking how he would earn his money. "God will provide," he repeated.

The next day, two thieves raided a caravan and made off with a bag of gold. They wanted to hide it for a time. It was too heavy to carry, so they rented the man's donkey for an amount equal to a week's labor. They put the gold bags on the donkey and went to a field. They had agreed to divide the loot, but both had second thoughts. The shorter one poisoned the food of the other. Before eating it, the taller one stabbed the shorter one. He then sat down to lunch and died on the second bite. The donkey, still carrying its gold, returned to the owner, who was suddenly a rich man.

You have already been of great help, Dr. Ecco. We can wait while you unearth the election gold or you can cooperate with us directly. Tell us where the ballots are. We think that Rose's note in the Oregonian contains a clue.

We are prepared to pay you a very large sum for the answer. You do take fees for solving puzzles, don't you, Dr. Ecco? Just name your price.

The ticket agent at the counter will take any response you have.

In service of the Lord,
Warriors of the Rapture

Ecco handed me the letter. After I finished reading, he said with a wink, "It's true, I do take fees, don't I?"

He sat down to write. All I saw were the words "$50,000 now, the rest later." Ecco put this into a sealed envelope and handed it to the woman at the ticket counter. She nodded and smiled. He looked at me: "Just trying to make a living . . ."

I started to protest, but he just raised his hand. "For the next week, Professor, you can observe me all you want, but don't ask me any questions."

When we arrived in Portland, Ecco went immediately to an Internet café and looked up information about summer activities on Hood River. "What could he be up to?" I wondered.

From the café, we drove to the offices of the *Oregonian*. "My name is Jacob Ecco," Ecco said to the editor, who met us at the receptionist's desk. "This is my friend and colleague, Professor Scarlet. We are sorry to have asked you to stay late."

"The omniheurist himself!" said the editor with a smile, shaking our hands. "We've been eagerly awaiting you. It is a pleasure to meet you, too, Professor Scarlet. Of course we know of your previous exploits, Dr. Ecco. My name is Jimmy Lyons. Please come to my office. We need privacy."

"Your office may be a bad place to meet," Ecco replied. "Could we meet in your basement instead? I need your senior editors and your two best photographers."

"Do you think we're bugged?" asked Lyons, surprised. Ecco did not reply..

Once we were all in the basement, Ecco began by addressing Lyons himself. "Are you willing to help me get to the bottom of this mystery? It involves major election fraud and maybe the fate of the entire country. I don't deny it will be risky."

"Risk is part of the job," Lyons replied. "We will help. What do you need?"

"Does anyone know how to drive really fast?" Ecco asked.

"Sam Johnson," they all answered. Sam, the photographer, was in his early 20s. "Sam, wouldn't you like to match your over-powered Ford against any pursuer?" Lyons asked. Sam smiled and nodded.

"I also need an expert cyclist," Ecco said.

"How about Jake Wren?" Lyons replied. As if on signal, Jake did a standing somersault, smiled, and nodded.

A few other reporters joined in. "Colleagues, we are going to take a drive next week and maybe a few others afterward," said Ecco. "I will be looking for clues on each drive. I may or may not find what we're looking for. If you are willing to do this, you must put yourself at my complete disposition. If I seem to fail, please bear with me. On each drive, please carry a shovel. Johnson, I want you to photograph anyone who is following us. Jake, you should have your fold-up bike always in your trunk. Agreed?"

All nodded. As the group started to break up, a section editor approached. "And Dr. Ecco, we have a question for you."

Are There Spies?

"HERE'S THE PROBLEM, Dr. Ecco," the section editor said. "Our editor-in-chief, Jimmy Lyons, has been told anonymously that our newspaper had been infiltrated by editorial spies. He's not sure whether it is true. Rumors of threats have also been circulating, so none of us want to be identified with this assertion.

"Suppose that three of us think there really are spies. Two disagree. Still, all five of us agree that Lyons should understand that at least three, but not all, of us think there are spies. We call these the Three Spy and Some NoSpy conditions, respectively. We also agree that Lyons should not learn what any of us think. We call this the Anonymity condition.

"We know Lyons will interview each of us individually and will only be satisfied with a statement that refers to the person questioned and at most two other people. We call this the Limited Reference condition. That is, Lyons won't accept generalities such as 'At least three out of all five people think there are spies.' He will think that is just hearsay.

"Instead he wants statements like 'of Ellen, Daniel, and me, at least two think there are spies' or 'of Arthur and me, at least one thinks there are no spies.' He is happy to hear more than one statement from a person as long as it follows this rule."

Warm-up: What can they say to prove Three Spy and Some NoSpy while satisfying the Anonymity and Limited Reference conditions?

Solution to warm-up: Let's call the editorial heads A, B, C, D, and E based on the first letter of their names. Assume that A, C, and D think there are spies. Suppose that A and B both say: "At least one of A and B thinks there are spies." D and E each say: "At least two of C, D, and E think there are spies." C says: "At least one of A, B, and C thinks there are no spies." The first two statements ensure that at least three think there are spies (Three Spy). The last ensures that at least one thinks there are none (Some NoSpy). In these circumstances, either A or B could think there are spies and any of C, D, or E could think there are none (Anonymity).

1. Under the same rules from Lyons and with the same goal, could we prove that EXACTLY three of the five people think there are spies? If so, how? If not, why not?

2. Again under the same rules and with the same goal, could we prove that EXACTLY four people think there are spies? If so, how? If not, why not?

3. Would your answer to question 2 change if we had only to prove that AT LEAST four of the five people think there is a spy?"

After solving these problems, we left. "Here is a nice generalization, Professor Scarlet," said Ecco. "For which group sizes S, numbers B in that group who suspect a spy with Reference Limit L, is it possible to prove to Lyons that at least (alternatively, exactly) B people think there is a spy while preserving the Anonymity and the Some NoSpy conditions?" This problem is still open.

That night we checked into the Benson Hotel. Ecco had reserved a suite.

Day 1: We went out in a line of five cars. At several points along the road Ecco stopped the convoy. Once, he dug with a shovel. Discovering nothing, Ecco, eyes downcast, shook his head and returned to our car. We circled back to the *Oregonian* headquarters. During our entire trip, a blue sedan followed us, even stopping when we stopped. The cross and the fire of the Warriors of the Rapture were printed on a flag flying from the car antenna. Sam Johnson took pictures of the car in full view of the drivers. They didn't mind.

"Did you notice the two Pontiacs without any markings that also trailed us, circling whenever we stopped?" Ecco asked me later. I shook my head. "Try to notice tomorrow."

Late that evening, I heard two knocks on the door. When I opened it, I saw nobody, but a gym bag was lying on the floor. I brought it in and showed it to Ecco. We unzipped it to find five piles, each containing a hundred $100 bills. The note accompanying the money said: "Here's the money you wanted, Ecco, compliments of Elmer Nuth. We are watching you carefully. God is with us."

Ecco soaked the money in a light Woolite solution and put it into a plastic hotel bag.

Day 2: We went all the way to the Dalles east on Highway 84. Ecco asked us to go late at night. Again we were followed. Again, Ecco stopped the car several times to look on the side of the road, at one point asking for help to dig a large hole—once again nothing. He shook his head. The reporters looked at one another in disbelief. I wondered what he was looking for. Could Rose's puzzle stump even Ecco? I missed Evangeline.

Day 3: Day off. We did not drive during the day. That night, Ecco asked me to turn on the television and not to let anyone in for any reason. He put on a dark wig that masked his distinctive red hair. He took the plastic bag of money, put it into a coat, and disappeared down a service exit. When he returned, I asked him where he had been. "Flyboys," he said. He gave no further explanation.

Day 4: Another drive. This time to Hood River. Same result, except that I now could count the cars following us: the same number as we had.

"Are we any closer to finding the ballots?" I asked Ecco when we were alone.

"Physically, no, but spiritually, yes," Ecco said with a relaxed smile. "And we have to think probabilistically. Let me share with you a nice puzzle in that regard."

Calculating the Odds

SEEMING TO FORGET the drama and danger surrounding us, Ecco started right in: "If two fair coins, a dime and a penny, are flipped, and you are told that the dime comes up heads, then what is the likelihood that the penny comes up heads as well? Obviously $\frac{1}{2}$.

"On the other hand, if you are told that two coins are flipped and at least one is heads, then there is only a $\frac{1}{3}$ chance that the other is heads."

"Seems strange," I said.

"It seems paradoxical," Ecco continued. "But there is a simple way to understand this. First consider the possible outcomes before you know anything about the flipped values. Represent a dime landing on heads as Dh; a dime landing on tails as Dt; and similarly for the penny: Ph and Pt.

"There are four possibilities:

    Dh Ph
    Dh Pt
    Dt Ph
    Dt Pt

"Initially, all four possibilities have the same probability. If you are told that at least one is heads, then you are left with these possibilities:

Dh Ph
Dh Pt
Dt Ph

"all of which are equally likely. In only one of these three cases are there two heads. So, a tails is more likely for the other coin.

"But before letting your students book a trip to Vegas, note that if, instead of being told that one coin has landed on heads, you are told that the dime has landed on heads, then two possibilities remain:

Dh Ph
Dh Pt

"and each has the same likelihood. Knowing the value of the dime doesn't help you guess the value of the penny.

"The key to unraveling such apparent paradoxes is to characterize the initial set of possibilities (initial meaning before you receive any extra information) and then to eliminate possibilities based on that extra information.

"Here is a different-sounding problem for which this method works. There are four socks in a drawer, two red and two blue. They all feel the same to the touch.

"If you choose two without looking at them, what are the chances they will be of the same color? To understand this, it is best to give

labels to each sock—Ra and Rb for the red socks, and Ba and Bb for the blue socks. We don't finally care which red sock we get or which blue one, but this allows us to lay out the probabilities precisely. So, we can get (in order from left to right):

Ra Rb
Ra Ba
Ra Bb
Rb Ra
Rb Ba
Rb Bb
Ba Bb
Ba Rb
Ba Ra
Bb Ba
Bb Ra
Bb Rb

"All of these are equally likely, but only four of these 12 choices lead to the desired outcome. We can also approach this in a more abstract way. There is a probability of $\frac{1}{2}$ that my first sock is red and in that case the likelihood that my next sock is red is $\frac{1}{3}$, because only one of the remaining three socks is red. So the probability of two reds is $\frac{1}{6}$. Similarly, the probability of two blues is $\frac{1}{6}$. Adding these up (because they are mutually exclusive), we get $\frac{1}{3}$."

1. Suppose I tell you the first sock is blue. Then what is the chance you get a pair of blue socks? Suppose I tell you that at least one sock of a pair is blue. Then what is the chance they both are?

"In case socks lack sufficient glamour," Ecco said, "let's return to a gambling scenario (that's closer to our ballot problem, anyway): there are five opaque boxes. Two contain $10,000 and the others contain the same weight in green paper. So, from the outside, they are indistinguishable. You are allowed to choose a single box, and of course you want one with $10,000. Your adversary knows which boxes contain the money.

"Here are the rules of the game. You point to a box. Your adversary must open two other boxes that have no money. There are now three unopened boxes, including the one you pointed to originally. You may now switch your choice."

2. Do you switch or not? Calculate the probabilities and see.

3. Suppose your adversary opens only one moneyless box. Do you switch in that case? The same simple method works.

4. If you know a family has two kids and at least one is a girl, what is the chance that the other is a girl? Does this change if you know a family has two kids and you see one playing outside and it is a girl?

I couldn't understand Ecco's good mood that Wednesday morning. "We're going to relax this evening," he said. We had dinner, and then took a walk. A car drove by and someone flipped an envelope in our direction.

> Ecco,
>
> It's not been safe for me to observe you closely, but I hope you know what you're doing. Rose is in danger. They are checking every possible friend she might have—artist, climber, windsurfer—everyone from St. Helens to Bend and from Goldendale to Newport. They roughed up her climbing friend Scot pretty badly, but he didn't know where she was hiding. Hurry, please hurry.
>
> B

"Race against time," Ecco muttered, ripping up the note. Then he fell silent. By Thursday morning, he seemed in good spirits again, but all he said was, "Let's go. We have things to do today."

Day 5: Thursday afternoon. Our caravan went to Hood River in the late afternoon. In the evening, we attended the Families in the Park event. The reporters seemed restless, but sat quietly. The show began with musicians and dancers. To my great surprise, Evangeline gave a Tiger Gung Fu performance. She was lit up by a spotlight. During her performance, two red-haired kids ran by us, seeming to pick up something. But I couldn't be sure in the weak light.

After the performance was finished, Ecco invited all the reporters over for cupcakes. Evangeline joined us. He gave a specific cupcake to each person. Inside the wrapping was a piece of paper. "Keep chatting and read," he said in a low voice.

"Are you sure about these instructions?" Lyons asked.

"I've been sure since the first day," Ecco said. "You just lose them. We walk out with beers in our hands. We want to give the impression that there is no work going on tonight. Are you ready?"

They all nodded. Ecco, Evangeline, and I went north across the Hood River Bridge and east on Highway 14. Lyons started back west on Route 84. Jake Wren took his bike up the old highway. Sam Johnson went south on Highway 35.

As we drove over the bridge, I asked Ecco how he planned to shake our pursuers. "Each of us has only one now," he said. "And they are running low on air, thanks to the twins."

Sure enough, our pursuing Pontiac had slowed down and the drivers got out to look at their tires. Ecco chuckled..

"Yes," he said. "I guess they're completely out of air."

We drove across the Hood River bridge into Washington and then headed east. The desert rocks looked particularly dark and menacing in the darkening sky. A few miles past the bridge, Ecco's phone rang. "Are you clear?" Ecco asked. "Then dig. When the copters arrive, tell them 'Dufur.'"

We drove to the Washington State side of the Dalles bridge. Ecco and

Evangeline lay quietly on a rock, side by side, gazing at the night stars, but I paced around nervously, watching every car to see if it would stop. Thirty minutes later, a plane flew by overhead. It blinked its lights.

"Our work is done," Ecco announced. "Now we can relax. I know a windsurfing shed where we can hide for a few days."

Day 6: The front page of the *Oregonian* featured a story that began a firestorm.

Rose's Ballots Demand Investigation

Here are photographs of some of the punched ballots provided to us by Rose Edwards. Our labs in Washington State have determined that the ballots are of the type and manufacture of those used in Ohio. The format and the age are correct. We demand a full investigation of how these punched ballots disappeared from the election officials' buildings. How many other ballots were involved?

Day 7: The counter-accusations began immediately.. Here was an editorial published by a small newspaper in the Dalles. "You can't prove these were punched by voters," it read. "In fact, the county has in its ballot boxes exactly as many ballots as people who signed in that morning. This is simply a fabrication. . . . Your candidate lost the election. Deal with it. It's un-American to question the process. The *Oregonian* should fire its editorial board—or we will do it for you."

Day 8: The *Oregonian* hired extra security. The wires picked up the story, but only as a controversy. Editors formed investigative reporting teams, though.

Day 10: Paul Hayes of Cuyahoga County stepped forward. "I kind of suspected things might not be right, so I left a little smidgen of blood on my ballot when I voted."

A few tense days followed. Analysis found the blood on one of Rose's ballots. It matched Hayes's DNA.

Day 14: The story dominated the news. But the election's winners struck back. "It's all a forgery," reported one talk show host. "The *Oregonian* ballots have nothing to do with the election."

Day 16: The residents of Cuyahoga took to the streets—an entire cross-section of the population—students, janitors, engineers, factory workers, dentists, working Moms and soccer Moms, rich and poor. **We Protest Election Fraud; Sincere Revote Now** read their banners. The sincere revote idea was for each person who actually voted on election day to vote again in the same way that he or she had voted on that day.

Day 21: The election commission accepted a sincere revote for one week later.

Day 28: The numbers came out a lot closer to the *Oregonian* counts than to the ones reported by the machines.

The rest is a matter of public record: the string of Sincere Revotes, the resignations, the sting when the leading members of the Warriors of the Rapture were captured while placing explosives in the basement of the *Oregonian*, and the widespread admissions of fraud, under promise of amnesty, among election officials.

Baskerhound was cleared of all wrongdoing after Rose described how she had come to jump off the bridge. Kate and the twins returned from Alaska.

Lessons from the Boy Who Cried Wolf

WE WERE IN a celebratory mood when Ecco gathered us back at the MacDougal Street apartment. "I don't understand what you did," I said.

"Well, there were several parts that had to work out," Ecco allowed. "The most intellectually challenging part was to decrypt Rose's message. I was stumped until you came in with Baskerhound's note. Turns out that hint was due to the twins. They had cracked Rose's *Oregonian* message too."

"I still never understood why that hint helped you so much," I said.

Ecco smiled. "Yes, I know. Anyway, then there was the little matter of delivering the ballots without anyone's getting hurt.

"One problem was how to respond to the Warriors of the Rapture. I knew that they hadn't cracked the code. If they had, they wouldn't have harassed us at the airport. So, I told them what they wanted to hear: I didn't know where the ballots were, either. Even better, I behaved as they thought I would—as an omniheurist for hire. That's why I asked them for a $50,000 advance, most of which is in the hands of some intrepid night-flying helicopter pilots right now.

"But I'm getting ahead of myself. I knew that the Warriors would follow us wherever we went. I needed safety in numbers. That's why I appealed to the *Oregonian*. It's a first-rate newspaper. I was confident their reporters would be willing to take risks for a story of this importance.

"But I still needed an element of surprise. Many think the best way to achieve surprise is to do the completely unexpected. But that would overestimate human nature. To surprise someone, conform to his or her expectations a few times, three or four at most. Then violate those expectations suddenly and completely.

"You remember our drives. Each day I examined the side of the road; some days I dug, but I didn't find anything. They didn't expect me to be able to crack the code, so my failure to find anything conformed to their expectations. I knew it was working when I saw the look in my best friend's face after the third day."

He smiled at me. I looked sheepishly at the ground.

Ecco continued, "It really is human nature. On the surface, the lesson of the *Boy Who Cried Wolf* story is not to raise a false alarm, but the deeper lesson is that people are easily convinced that alarms are false. Our convoy of omniheurists and reporters went out several times without result. We seemed to give up when we went to the Families in the Park festival.

"At the festival, we spread blankets and sat down to a picnic. Our pursuers became careless. They watched the show, too. You remember when two kids ran by and picked up a box. That was Eli and Cloe. They placed sharpened jacks under our pursuers' car wheels. Our pursuers also didn't know that the old Columbia River highway isn't open to modern cars a few miles east of Hood River. It's blocked by a gate. Jake Wren had his bike, of course.

"But getting away from them was only one part of the problem. The other part was to get the ballots to the *Oregonian*. Driving back to Portland would invite interception.

"The night I snuck away in that ridiculous wig, I went to the Portland Downtown Heliport and contracted with several pilots to pick the ballots up and take them to an airstrip on a farm near Dufur. The ballots then went on by plane. Unlike the donkey in the parable, the pilots went where I told them to fly. Do you think the Warriors will appreciate the good cause to which their money has gone?"

Fair Counts

NO LONGER WORRIED about being pursued, Ecco invited Baskerhound and Kate's family to MacDougal Street.

"I've asked you over to brainstorm this question of verifiable elec-
tions," Ecco began. "Paper ballots cannot be enough. The Cuyahoga
affair showed how easy it was to replace one paper ballot by another.
Paul Hayes was exceptional. Very few people will shed blood on their
ballots. Besides, doing so eliminates all hope of anonymity."

"What are our objectives, then?" asked Cloe.

"Here's a start," Ecco said.

1. Every vote is counted as cast. No ballot is replaced (fraudulently
   or not) by a different one.

2. Exactly those people who vote on election day have their votes
   counted. It should not be possible to stuff ballot boxes with ghost
   votes.

3. Each voter can choose to preserve his or her anonymity. Paul Hayes
   didn't so choose, but most people do.

4. If a voter charges fraud, he or she should be able to document that charge convincingly, even if he or she doesn't have absolute proof.

5. A voter should not normally be able to demonstrate how he or she voted to prevent vote selling.

"And our assumptions?" Cloe asked.

"People sign in as they enter the polling place," Ecco began, "so the total number of ballots can't exceed the number of signatures. Also, we'll assume that a single individual can vote in only one place. Violating this assumption on a large scale involves many people and invites prison time."

"In the right circumstances, we can also assume that handwriting can't be forged," Baskerhound added. "Photocopying may reproduce colors, but handwriting also changes the three-dimensional features of the writing surface,"

"I agree," Ecco said. "Also, I think that if it comes to a recount, there are trustworthy organizations like the League of Women Voters who will recount fairly. The challenge is to put the correct ballots in their hands.

"Now let's consider some solutions: Number the ballots and reprint the number on a tab separated by a perforation. The voter takes the tab upon leaving. If there is a recount, each voter can check that his or her numbered ballot is there."

"But what if the bad guys printed two ballots with the same number?" young Eli pointed out.

"Right," said Baskerhound. "Suppose that in addition to a detachable tab with a ballot number, the ballot itself had a signature field. I could then sign the ballot or even spit on it."

"That destroys anonymity," Ecco pointed out, "but the idea is a start. Instead of a signature field, we'll have a 'scribbling' field. I can write anything I like in the scribbling field: random numbers, a common expression (e.g., 'A day at the beach'), anything that is hard to copy precisely but that doesn't identify me."

Ecco paused. "Can you see what we can do with this?" he asked.

We all thought about it for a time, but gave up.

Ecco continued: "Suppose further that ballots can be constructed with backing paper, reminiscent of carbon copies, so that if a person writes something on the ballot, his or her writing is traced onto the backing paper. Both the ballot and the backing paper should be designed to be pressure-sensitive, so pressing harder on the ballot will make a deeper impression on the backing paper. The backing paper may lie behind the whole ballot or only a portion of it. It should not be possible to write directly on the backing paper after it has been ripped off. Is this enough?"

1. Can you extend this to a verifiable voting method?

Ecco presented his solution. I shook my head slowly with a smile—such an elegant idea. Baskerhound gave the greatest praise: "So simple, it could work," he said with a chuckle.

"I hope that's the last any of us will have to do with political intrigue for a while," Ecco responded as he reached his hand toward Kate, who clasped it and smiled.

Solutions

1. Harout will never use Michael without some added assumption, no matter how many gold coins he has. To see why, consider the following inductive argument. From the warm-up, we know that Harout would not use Michael for his last one, two, three, or four coins. Suppose Harout would not use Michael for his last k or fewer coins but will for $k + 1$ coins. Consider his thinking. Sending one coin is pointless, because Michael will take it. Sending all $k + 1$ coins gives Michael no incentive to be honest. Suppose Harout sends some number m in between: $1 < m < k + 1$. Harout can imagine Michael's reasoning as follows: "Even if I'm honest, Harout will use the insured carrier the next time because the number remaining will be less than k. So I might as well steal these m coins."

2. For 10 coins under the trust-until-cheated protocol, Harout will prepare packets of size 4, then 3, then 2, then 1. Assuming Michael is honest every time, Harout will see 6 coins get to Zurich with 4 going to the smuggler. It's not in Michael's interest to cheat at any time because he'll never get more than 4 by doing so.

3. For 20 coins, Harout will set up lots of size 5, 5, 4, 3, 2, and 1. The smuggler will receive 6 coins if he is honest and no more in any other case.

4. For 50 coins, Harout will set up 5, 9, 8, 7, 6, 5, 4, 3, 2, 1. The smuggler Michael will get 10 of these coins. Dishonesty will not help him.

5. Assume that Michael would prefer to be dishonest (when profits are equal) in order to exact revenge on Harout, and Harout knows this. For 10 coins, the lots become 3, 3, 2, 2. Harout will get 5 to Zurich and Michael will get 5. For 20, the lots will be 4, 5, 4, 3, 2, and 2. The smuggler will get 7 and Harout will get 13 delivered to Zurich. For 50, the lots will be 4, 9, 8, 7, 6, 5, 4, 3, 2, and 2. The smuggler will receive 11 and 39 will be delivered to Zurich.

Here is how to calculate the lot sizes when Michael prefers to be honest. (I had a complex method involving dynamic programming, but Peter Carpenter showed me a much more elegant one.) The last lot Harout sends should consist of 1 coin. If he sends more coins at the end, Michael will certainly steal them. The next-to-last lot should have 2, then 3, and so on. This tells us how many to send if Harout's initial coin collection is 1 coin, or 3 coins, or 6, 10, 15, 21, 28, 36 . . . coins. These "perfect coin numbers" are derived from the series $1, 1 + 2, 1 + 2 + 3, 1 + 2 + 3 + 4, \ldots$ If Harout has $1 + 2 + 3 + \ldots + n$ coins initially, then he divides them into lots of size n, $n - 1$, $n - 2, \ldots, 1$ and sends in descending order. If Harout's initial collection is not perfect, then his first lot is the number that will reduce his collection size to the next lower perfect coin number. For example, if he has 31 coins, his first lot will consist of 3 coins.

If Michael prefers to be dishonest when profits are equal, then the argument becomes somewhat more complex. This can be solved using "dynamic programming" and "recursion." If you are familiar with these concepts, then give it a try, perhaps after following the hints below. If you are not, then you get something very close by following Peter Carpenter's approach: given n coins, divide the lots based on the Michael-the-good-guy model for $n - 1$ coins and then send 1 coin at the end.

Hints for the dynamic programming approach:

a. Let Merchant(n) = the number the merchant will get from the last n coins if the smuggler has been honest until that point and the merchant plays optimally.

b. Smuggler(n) = the number he will get from the last n coins assuming the merchant follows the merchant's optimal strategy.

The function try(n,k) determines what will happen when k are sent from the remaining n. If the smuggler will make at least as much from stealing the k as from taking a commission of 1 plus whatever the smuggler would earn from the merchant's strategy for $n - k$, then the smuggler will steal. Otherwise, he won't.

We can define the value of try(n,k) thus:

If $k \geq [1 + \text{Smuggler}(n - k)]$, then the smuggler will steal the k. The merchant will deliver $(n - k) \div 2$ more to Zurich than he has already sent and the smuggler will receive the k he has stolen in addition to whatever he has received as commission.

Otherwise, the smuggler won't steal. The merchant will then deliver $k - 1$ on the current trip plus the value of Merchant($n - k$). The smuggler will gain 1 for this trip plus the value of Smuggler($n - k$).

This suggests the following algorithm: initialize Merchant(0) = 0 and Smuggler(0) = 0. Also Merchant(1) = 0 and Smuggler(1) = 1 (because Harout will send his last coin with Michael if Michael has been honest up to that point). We are going to build up from there.

Suppose we have computed Merchant and Smuggler up to $n - 1$. To figure out what the Merchant should do when he has n coins and the Smuggler has been honest up to that point, imagine that the Merchant evaluates try(n,k) for every k from 1 to $n - 1$. The Merchant then chooses what is best for him.

This guarantees an optimal division of lots. For example, with 12 coins initially, the lots would be 4, 3, 2, 2, 1. Michael will deliver the 4, the 3, and the first 2, but won't deliver the second 2, so Harout will send the last lot by insured carrier.

The Pirates' Cantilever

1. You might think that you want the lightest on top and the heaviest on the bottom, but it turns out you want just the opposite. You put the 1-meter plank on the bottom, then the 2-meter plank, then the 3-meter plank, all the way up to the 10-meter plank. The 10-meter plank extends out a little more than 10.06 meters.

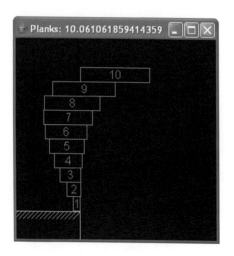

See if you can work out even better numbers.

2. When several planks can lie on a single one, one can extend out to nearly 13 meters.

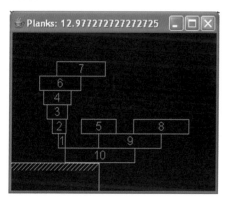

These solutions are due to Mike Birken. Mike explains his solution to this second problem as follows: "My goal was to use the 3 longest planks to reach out as far as possible from the table edge. I started by treating plank 10 like a balance scale, with planks 1 to 7 on the left side and planks 8 and 9 on the right. The largest value that can be moved from the left stack to the right stack while keeping the left stack heavier than the right is 5. I used plank 5 to counterbalance the weight of plank 8 on 9. The final stacks enabled me to push plank 10 a little more than halfway off the table. To make the solution more interesting, the stacking order of the left stack was intentionally selected to appear as precarious as possible, though mathematically stable."

SOLUTION TO
Cornering the Market

1. There are six identical goods. Let us say David bids up to x for the initial good and then $100,000 - x$ for the second. Then Goliath must win $N - 1$ times against either x or $100,000 - x$. David will make this as hard as possible, so $x = 100,000 - x = 50,000$. Therefore, if there are six items, Goliath must be prepared to beat $50,000 five times, so must have $255,000. When Goliath has only $200,000, David will get his supplies.

2. Suppose that David bids $33,000 every time until he has three machines. Goliath must stop him with a bid of $34,000 and must do so seven times. But $7 \times \$34,000 = \$238,000$, which is more than Goliath has, so David will get his machines.

3. Suppose Goliath bids $1,000 more than David, up to $31,000. Suppose David gets the first machine for $31,000, by bidding that amount before Goliath does. If David has $100,000, then Goliath has to bid $70,000 from then on, costing him $100,000 more than if he bid $51,000 five times, as he would have done if he had known David had $100,000. If Goliath wins with $31,000, then he knows that David has at least $30,000. If David had been known to have exactly that amount, then Goliath would have needed to spend $5 \times \$16,000$

= $80,000 to thwart David. Goliath therefore can afford to spend up to $37,000 four times and stay within a $180,000 budget. Suppose therefore Goliath bids up to $37,000. If David bids $38,000, then Goliath must meet all remaining bids, but now the worst case isn't even as relatively expensive for Goliath as before.

Close Enough

1. Here is a solution that requires only 5 swaps for

9	8	7	1	4	3	5	6	2	

   1   2   3   4   5   6   7   8   9

(start): 9 8 7 1 4 3 5 6 2

  (1,9): 2 8 7 1 4 3 5 6 9
  (2,7): 2 5 7 1 4 3 8 6 9
  (2,4): 2 1 7 5 4 3 8 6 9
  (3,8): 2 1 6 5 4 3 8 7 9
  (3,6): 2 1 3 5 4 6 8 7 9

2. For this initial configuration

     3 5 6 7 8 1 9 2 4

6 swaps are sufficient. Here is one method to put it into a 1-away configuration:

         3 5 6 7 8 1 9 2 4
(5,9): 3 5 6 7 4 1 9 2 8
         (The 4 and 8 are now close enough.)
(1,3): 6 5 3 7 4 1 9 2 8
(1,6): 1 5 3 7 4 6 9 2 8
         (The 4, 8, 1, 3, and 6 are now close enough.)
(2,4): 1 7 3 5 4 6 9 2 8
(7,8): 1 7 3 5 4 6 2 9 8
(2,7): 1 2 3 5 4 6 7 9 8

Can you do better?

3. Here is a very bad initial configuration for 9 items:

    8 9 1 2 3 4 5 6 7

Each element is 2 away from its correct position. Each swap can do no better than move a single sculpture into its correct position. Yet once the first 7 sculptures are in place, the last 2 will be only 1 away, so 7 moves is the worst case.

4. Omniheurist Tom Rokicki came up with the following beautiful solution (my colleague Richard Cole and mathematician Ivan Rezanka had similar intuitions).

One maximally bad initial configuration when the goal is to achieve a d-away configuration is to start with a $d + 1$ rotation from the in-order configuration. For example, when $d = 1$, the configuration 8 9 1 2 3 4 5 6 7 is a 2-rotation. By contrast, a 6-rotation (useful to maximize the number of swaps when the goal is to achieve a 5-away configuration) on 9 elements yields: 4 5 6 7 8 9 1 2 3.

Rokicki observed that there will be $n - (d + 1)$ numbers that are at least $d + 1$ out of place (1, 2, 3 in the 6-rotation example), all in the same direction. Each swap can move only a single one of those numbers into range of its location. Swapping them into place in order (for this example, swapping the 1 at position 7 with the 4 at position 1, then the 2 at position 8 with the 5 at position 2, and so on) is in fact an optimal solution.

In fact, no matter which initial configuration one starts with, one can swap 1 into place, then 2, then 3, and so on up to the largest $d + 1$ sculptures. Those last ones are no more than d away from their proper places.

5. How many 1-away configurations are there for n elements?

Recall the Fibbonaci sequence that seems to come up in so much of mathematics:

$$1, 1, 2, 3, 5, 8, 13, 21, 34, \ldots$$

Each number is the sum of the two previous ones, i.e., $\text{fib}(k + 2) = \text{fib}(k + 1) + \text{fib}(k)$. Let's identify the numbers by their position in that list, so $\text{fib}(0) = \text{fib}(1) = 1$, $\text{fib}(6) = 13$ (remember we're starting from 0), and so on. Well, the number of 1-away arrangements (including the perfectly sorted one) of n elements is just $\text{fib}(n)$.

> For $n = 1$, there is clearly just one ($\text{fib}(1)$).
> For $n = 2$, there are two: 1 2 and 2 1.
> For $n = 3$, there are three: 1 2 3; 1 3 2; 2 1 3
> For $n = 4$, there are five: three that involve 2 3 4 with 1 fixed; then swap the 1 and 2 and there are two arrangements of 3 and 4.

In general, there are $\text{fib}(n - 1)$ permutations of length n with the first sculpture in place. If the first sculpture is not in place it must be at position 2, but this means the second sculpture must be in position 1 (no other element can be in position 1). So this fixes the first two positions out of order. Now there are there are fib($n - 2$) permutations of the last $n - 2$ sculptures.

This last result was first discovered in the following nicely written article (in French) that you can find on the Web: "Quelques résultats dans la métrique des permutations," by René Lagrange.

SOLUTION TO
Gold in the Balance

1, 2, and 3. We will answer question 2 first. This will give us answers to questions 1 and 3. It may seem surprising at first, but when the balance point is at the Leftmost Balance Point, then the Leftmost Balance Point is the Leading Edge

Left Point is to the left of Leading Edge.

Left Point is to the right of Leading Edge.

Left Point is to the right of Leading Edge.

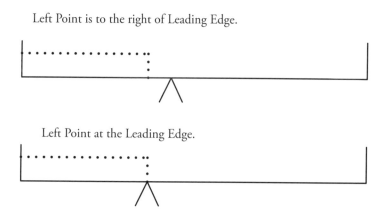

Left Point at the Leading Edge.

Balance and Gold Dust Solution:
When balance point is at Left Point, Leading Edge is at
Left Point, too.

Here's why. (It helps to remember using a seesaw.) Suppose the Leftmost Balance Point were to the left of the Leading Edge. Then removing the last bit of gold dust would cause the trough to tip left, implying that the balance point has to move farther left. This contradicts the notion of Leftmost Balance Point. Suppose the Leftmost Balance Point were to the right of the Leading Edge. Then adding gold dust would add more weight to the left of the Leftmost Balance Point, again implying the trough would tip left. Again, this would move the balance point farther left. So the Leftmost Balance Point must align with the Leading Edge. This answers question 1, because the Leftmost Balance Point is clearly to the left of the center of the trough, so the Leading Edge at that point must also be left of center. Nothing in our argument regarding question 2 depended on anything other than that the gold dust had a nonnegative weight, so this applies to the impurity question, too. Alan Siegel suggested the basis for this formulation of the solution.

4. Suppose that when the Leading Edge is at the Leftmost Balance Point, x centimeters have gold dust. The center of mass of the dust is $\frac{x}{2}$ and the weight is $10x$. The center of mass of the trough is at position 10 and the weight is 300. These two weights must balance one another about x. So $300\,(10 - x) = 5x^2$. That is $5x^2 + 300x - 3000 = 0$. Equivalently, $x^2 + 60x - 600 = 0$. $x = -30 + \frac{\sqrt{3600 + 2400}}{2} = \frac{17.46}{2} = 8.73$.

1. The beautiful symmetrical design shown in figure

7	6	5	4	3	2
8	7	6	5	4	3
9	8	7	6	5	4
10	9	8	7	6	5
11	10	9	8	7	6
12	11	10	9	8	7

gives the maximum possible happiness. This is a perfect zoning for all blocks.

2. Each block has at most four neighbors. Simply lay out the numbers in order, perhaps alternating left to right with right to left. That is, start as follows:

```
 1   2   3   4   5   6
12  11  10   9   8   7
13  14  15  16  17  18
24  23  22  21  20  19
25  26  27  28  29  30
36  35  34  33  32  31
```

Because each block has at least two good blocks and at most two bad ones, its net happiness must be nonnegative.

3. Consider a number in the middle. Say it is X. For it to have neighbors that all make it happy, it must be surrounded by all four of its numerical neighbors: $X - 1$, $X - 2$, $X + 1$, and $X + 2$, as shown below.

$$
\begin{array}{ccc}
 & (X - 2) & \\
(X - 1) & X & (X + 1) \\
 & (X + 2) &
\end{array}
$$

But now consider the situation of, say, $X - 1$. It should also be surrounded by its four numerical neighbors: $X - 2$, $X - 3$, X, and $X + 1$, but two of those (namely $X + 1$ and $X - 1$) are already taken.

4. Here is a design on all 36 numbers that gives a net happiness of 20. I don't know whether this is the best possible.

```
 1   2  23  24  25  26
 3   4  21  22  27  28
 5   6  19  20  29  30
 7   8  17  18  31  32
 9  10  15  16  33  34
11  12  13  14  35  36
```

Maybe you can come up with a nice layout algorithm for general shapes, population types, and likes and dislikes among those types. If so, I can think of a few cities and suburbs that surely could use your help.

Optimal Farming

DENIS BIRNIE OF New Zealand designs irrigation systems for a living. One of his observations: a single pivot arm can cover an entire square field. "On the end of the fixed pivot arm, there's another arm connected with an elbow joint whose length is about 41 percent of the main arm's length. When the end of the main arm is touching the middle of the field edge, the elbow is bent 90 degrees; when pointing at the field corners, the elbow is straight."

He went on to present the following solutions to the problem, which he has kindly allowed me to edit and use.

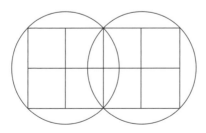

Thus Minimum Area = 3.14km² for $k = 2$ sprinklers (57% above the field's 2km² area).

Four smaller circles can replace one larger circle while still completely covering the desired/required square area:

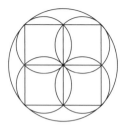

This has the interesting property of retaining the same total coverage area, but the nature of the excess (non-square) area has changed from being all external to the square to being half internal overlap and half external. Note also, that there is no triple overlap.

Thus Minimum Area = 3.14km² for any even k set of identical radii sprinklers which can be arranged in a 1:2 matrix (or any regular m by n grid matrix). For large k it is possible to make the external overlap small—at the expense of increased internal overlap. Now for the solutions to the questions.

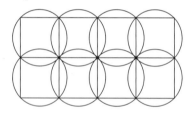

Question 1: $k = 5$ with varying radii.

By using one 707.11m radius and four 353.55m radius sprinklers it is possible to cover a total area of 3.14km². However, as shown there are two areas of triple overlap meaning approximately 0.11km² can be ignored for a final total area cost of 3.03km².

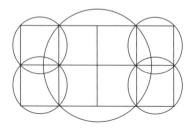

Question 2: $k = 5$ with identical radii.

To cover a square area of 2km² would require 5 sprinklers to each cover a 0.4km² area—thus the minimum radius is 447.2m. However as the field is not arranged 1:5 a larger radius is required.

Some experimentation found the coverage pattern shown to the right with an approximate radius of 530.3m giving a final cost for the brothers of ~4.29km². While there is a significant triple overlap the inefficiency of the double overlaps in this pattern is too high. (Alan Dragoo thinks there is a solution that covers just 4.11 km², but it's too complicated to present here.)

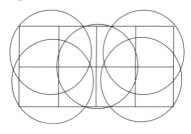

Question 3: increasing k (10, 20 100)?

As noted above where k allows a 1:2 matrix (or even grid) pattern the area is a constant 3.14km².

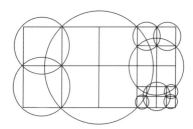

With certain k (5, 11,...) a fractal pattern as shown on the left can be used. This has a constant area of 3.03km² for the first few generations, but then as shown due to a total overlap by the sprinkler three generations up the "trunk" a sprinkler can be dropped! This pattern using 19 sprinklers ($r = 1 \times 500$m, 2×250m, 4×125m and 12×62.5m) has a cost to the brothers of approximately 3.01km^2.

So, depending on k and the pattern used the area is either constant at 3.14km^2 or tends towards some minimal value below 3km^2 (but well above 2km^2).

Smooth As Ice

1. Using techniques from computer science (notably A* search in order to search efficiently through many possible routings), Mike Birken and David Geldreich came up with a 35-move solution using one Zamboni.

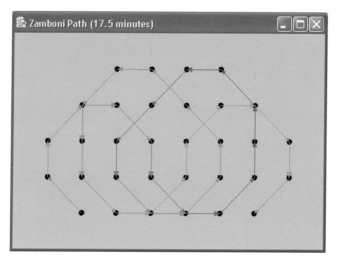

Zamboni Path (17.5 minutes)

2. Adam Spreight showed some four Zamboni solutions, where each Zamboni crossed only nine edges.

First he numbered the points as follows:

		01	02	03	04		
	05	06	07	08	09	10	
11	12	13	14	15	16	17	18
19	20	21	22	23	24	25	26
	27	28	29	30	31	32	

Then he proposed routes for each Zamboni.

$z1 = [29, 28, 27, 19, 11, 05, 06, 14, 22, 29]$
$z2 = [30, 31, 32, 26, 18, 10, 09, 15, 23, 30]$
$z3 = [27, 20, 12, 05, 01, 02, 08, 16, 24, 31]$
$z4 = [28, 21, 13, 07, 03, 04, 10, 17, 25, 32]$

Patton's Traffic Intersection

1. Only a single vehicle can be in the center at one time. It takes 1 minute for the first tank to enter. Starting with that one, 18 more tanks enter that square. After the last one enters, it has another 7 minutes to exit the rectangle. So the total time is 26 minutes.

2. Figure 4

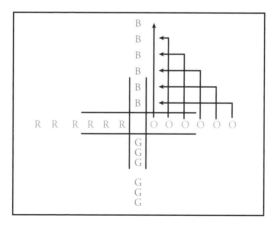

shows what each vehicle in the orange column (the Os) does in the first 6 minutes. The other vehicles all move symmetrically (so each vehicle moves first to its right, and then all but the head of the column move to their left). Figure 5 that follows

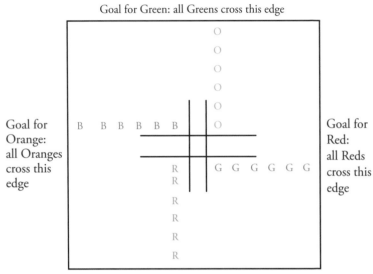

Goal for Green: all Greens cross this edge

Goal for Orange: all Oranges cross this edge

Goal for Red: all Reds cross this edge

Goal for Blue: all Blues cross this edge

shows the vehicles after each column has performed this 90-degree rotation. From that position, each vehicle travels directly to the far edge in another 7 minutes and crosses that edge in the 8th minute. This gives 14 minutes in all.

3. This is an optimal solution, because even if each vehicle took the most direct route possible (disregarding crashes), the last vehicle in each column would require 13 minutes to cross the far edge. But we know those last vehicles can't go directly to the far edge, because they would crash in the center. So the slowest of the last vehicles must take at least 14 minutes. The rotation solution above takes only 1 more minute than the impossible direct one, so it's optimal.

4. The setup changes just a little: the first five vehicles travel out to a depth of five. The last one is just behind the fifth as shown in figure 6

Goal for Green: all Greens cross this edge

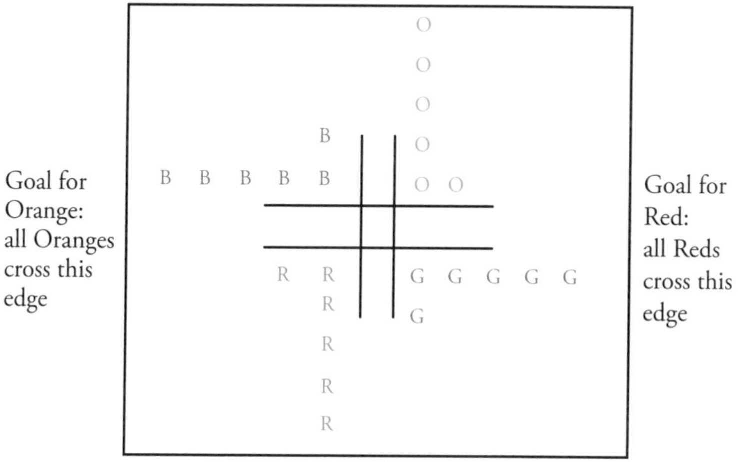

Goal for
Orange:
all Oranges
cross this
edge

Goal for
Red:
all Reds
cross this
edge

Goal for Blue: all Blues cross this edge

This near-rotation takes only 5 minutes. On the 8th minute, the two
that are in single file go ahead by two cells.

1. Yes, leave a black square empty next to (say, in a clockwise direction) every empty red square in the same concentric square. When red places a piece on a square, place a piece having a number one higher in the next empty position in a clockwise direction, unless the piece just placed is already covered by another black piece. In this figure

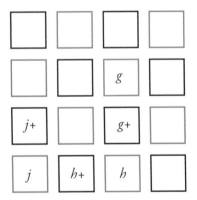

red piece h is covered by $h+$ (usually $h + 1$); red piece j is covered by $j+$ and g is covered by $g+$. Because $2n$ is a square number. This assures dominance by black.

2. No fixed k works. To see why, call two red squares (i,j) and (i',j') well separated if they share no black squares as neighbors and each has four black squares as neighbors. In figure

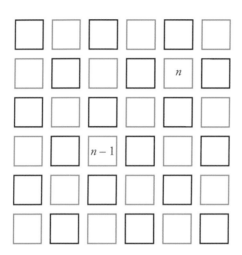

n and $n - 1$ are well separated.

Consider a collection of well-separated red squares and put the highest red pieces on them. The red square having n on it must have two black pieces neighboring it having numbers greater than n on them. The red square having $n - 1$ on it may have a black piece with n on it, but also another one greater than n. Each well-separated red square must, therefore, consume a black piece whose value is greater than n.

Note that the diagonals containing well-separated red squares (i) alternate between well-separated red squares and others; and (ii) must be surrounded by diagonals of red squares that have no well-separated red squares. Therefore, the number of well-separated red squares increases with $\frac{n}{4}$. Black must use $\frac{n}{2}$ pieces to cover those, half of those $(\frac{n}{4})$ must be greater than n, and the others must be at least $\frac{3n}{4}$. So, these $\frac{n}{2}$ black pieces must have greater values than any other red pieces. We call those black pieces the high dominators. Further, black can arrange it so that every empty red square is the neighbor of at least one high dominator. So any piece put on an empty (non-well-separated) red square can be covered by the high dominator already placed as a neighbor plus one other black piece having a value less than n. Therefore is $c + \frac{n}{4}$ where c is a small constant independent of n. In fact, Ecco conjectures that c is about 2. Can you do better?

Diamond Thieves

1. The answer is nine shipments. Notice first of all that anytime no theft takes place, at most two other shipments can determine which of the remaining middlemen, if any, is a thief. For example, if a shipment through M1 M2 M3 arrives safely, then two shipments through M1 M2 M4 and through M1 M2 M5 can settle the thievery status of each of M4 and M5. So if any of shipments 1 through 7 ends in success, we can surely finish in nine shipments. Let us call this the "Done in Two" argument.

Here are the middlemen used in the first four shipments.

    1: M1 M4 M5
    2: M2 M4 M5
    3: M3 M4 M5
    4: M1 M2 M3

If no theft occurs in any of these cases, then Done in Two applies. The first three thefts indicate that at least one of M4 and M5 is a thief. The last theft indicates that at least one of M1, M2, and M3 is a thief.

Here are the middlemen used in the next three shipments:

     5: M1 M2 M4
     6: M1 M3 M4
     7: M2 M3 M4

If any shipment ends without a theft, Done in Two applies. (In fact, we would know exactly who the thieves would be without any extra shipments: M5 and whichever of M1, M2, and M3 were not represented in the shipment.) Otherwise, M4 is certainly a thief and M5 is not. We proceed on that basis.

    Here are the middlemen used in the last two shipments:

     8: M1 M2 M5
     9: M1 M3 M5

If nothing is stolen when M1, M2, and M5 are the middlemen, then M3 and M4 are the thieves. Otherwise, either M1 or M2 is a thief. The last shipment determines whether it's M1 or M2.

    Ivan Rezanka has done extensive case analysis to demonstrate that nine is the best possible guarantee.

2. If we get feedback, then try the following in the first four shipments.

     1: M4 M1 M5
     2: M4 M2 M5
     3: M4 M3 M5
     4: M1 M2 M3

Assume there is a theft (otherwise the Done in Two argument applies) for every shipment. Then, as above, either M4 or M5 is a thief, as is one of M1, M2, and M3. Suppose that M4 is the thief. Then in at least two of the first three cases, M4 will be accused of being a thief. But M5 can also make this happen. This is just a hint.

Jam Session

1. We represent the 6 data bits followed by 4 check bits as follows:
$b1\ b2\ b3\ b4\ b5\ b6\ c1\ c2\ c3\ c4$

Here is one possibility of what the check bits could do:

> $c1$ is odd parity on $b1$, $b2$, $b3$, $b4$, $b5$, $b6$, $c1$, $c4$
> $c2$ is odd parity on $b1$, $b2$, $b3$, $b4$, $c3$, $c2$
> $c3$ is odd parity on $b1$, $b2$, $c1$, $c3$, $c4$
> $c4$ is odd parity on $b1$, $b5$, $b4$, $c4$

The trick is to ensure that different parity calculations differ depending on which bit has been flipped. If all the parities are correct, then no single bit has been flipped. If there is an error in b1, then the parities corresponding to $c1$, $c2$, $c3$, and $c4$ will all be bad.

Error in $b2$, then $c1$, $c2$, and $c3$ will be bad (first line below). The pattern continues.

> $b2$: $c1$, $c2$, $c3$
> $b3$: $c1$, $c2$
> $b4$: $c1$, $c2$, $c4$

$b5$: $c1$, $c4$
$b6$: $c1$
$c1$: $c1$, $c3$
$c2$: $c2$
$c3$: $c2$, $c3$
$c4$: $c3$, $c4$

John Trono notes that coding theorists would prefer to solve this problem using "Hamming codes," a technique whereby the 4 check bits are interspersed among the 6 data bits. Our spies are pragmatic, however, so any use of four check bits that identifies the error, if any, will do.

2. If you know that the offset between the bit flip to the first receiver and to the second is an odd number, then you can use:

$b1$, $b2$, $b3$, $b4$, $b5$, $b6$, $b7$, $b8$, Podd, Peven

where Podd ensures that there are an odd number of 1s among $b1$, $b3$, $b5$, $b7$, and Podd; and Peven ensures that there are an odd number of 1s among $b2$, $b4$, $b6$, $b8$, and Peven. Here is why this works: if no error is detected, then the data bits are correct. If the first receiver detects an error, say for Podd, then the second can detect an error only for Peven, because of the odd offset. Therefore, at least one of the two receivers will receive an error-free Podd group and at least one will receive an error-free Peven group. Headquarters will have to combine the results from the two receivers to determine the correct message packet.

3. If you know the offset is 4 bits, then Vlad Simionescu suggests a solution that uses just parity. The approach is simple: assign a single parity bit to the message. If the parity is consistent with the message m sent to at least one receiver, then m is correct. Otherwise the two receivers will differ in 2 bits at positions, say, i and $i + 4$ (technically, $i + 4$ mod 10, starting the numbering from 0). Because the sender sends first to the east receiver and next to the northwest receiver, bit i to the east receiver must be flipped and bit $i + 4$ to the northwest receiver must be flipped. So it is possible to look for inconsistencies in the two transmissions to figure out which bit is incorrect. Ivan Rezanka points out that a similar approach works for every offset except 5, provided the offset is known.

SOLUTION TO
Cruise Control

1. You need 6 kilometers. The harder cases occur when the car goes very fast. So we will concentrate on those. If you sense at kilometer 1 at 20.5 seconds and the car has already passed, then you knock out 30 kph to 170 kph. If you then sense at kilometer 2 at 26.6 seconds and the car has already passed, you knock out 180 kph to 270 kph. Then sense at kilometer 3 at 33.22 leaving either 280 kph to 320 kph (if the car hasn't passed) or 330 kph to 360 kph (if the car has). The first needs 3 more kilometers. The second needs only 2. No fewer than 6 is possible because there are more than 2^5 (32) possible answers.

2. You can net the fugitive in 6 kilometers or less even without deploying. The reason is that cars going fast can all be caught early on. This time, sense at kilometer 1 at 19.5 seconds. If you don't knock out 30 kph to 180 kph, then notice that there are just 16 possibilities left, and so the speed can be determined using 4 more kilometer sensors, at which point netting at 6 kilometers is no problem. So, let's say we still have 190 kph to 360 kph left. Again, sense at kilometer 2 at 26.6 seconds, leaving just 8 possibilities. If 190 kph to 270 kph are still possible (i.e., if the car hasn't passed), then 3 more kilometers are enough to catch the fugitive. So, let's say that we are left with speeds between 280 kph and 360 kph (i.e., the car has passed kilometer 2 by 26.6 seconds). Well, then we can net the car if we spring the net at 29.9 seconds. This is the best solution I know of if one cannot both deploy the net and access the sensor at the same kilometer.

3. Yes, much better. Just deploy the net at 6 seconds at kilometer 1 and you'll catch the car no matter what speed it travels in this range.

4. To handle continuous speeds, I will use the solution suggested by Tom Rokicki. His strategy is based on the following idea: "We always pop the netting to catch only the slowest speeds still possible, so the fugitive will never see the fence more than 10 seconds ahead of time."

The commands given to each sensor require a condition and several steps. The way Tom explains it, he starts with a possible range of speeds, says which kilometer it is, then says when to deploy the netting and when to fire the sensor. For example,

> Range 30.000..360.000 at 1 nettime 110.000 catches 30.000..32.727 sense 54.000 split 66.667

means: Given a range of speeds between 30 and 360, at kilometer 1, deploy the netting at time 110 seconds, catching cars going between 30 and 32.727; also fire up the sensor at time 54 seconds, which will split the speeds between those below 66.667 (if car has not been detected) and those above (if car has been detected).

Note that because of the range, the same kilometer will have two cases. So, for example, we have:

> Range 32.727..66.667 at 2 nettime 210.000 catches 32.727..34.286 sense 167.333 split 43.028, which is the speed range if the sensor at kilometer 1 found nothing.

We also have Range 66.667..360.000 at 2 nettime 98.000 catches 66.667..73.469 sense 55.000 split 130.909, if the sensor at kilometer 2 did find a car. If exactly equal, then take the first case.

Range 30.000..360.000 at 1 nettime 110.000 catches 30.000..32.727
sense 54.000
split 66.667
Range 30.000..360.000 at 1 nettime 110.000 catches 30.000..32.727
sense 54.000
split 66.667
Range 32.727..66.667 at 2 nettime 210.000 catches 32.727..34.286
sense 167.333
split 43.028
Range 34.286..43.028 at 3 nettime 305.000 catches 34.286..35.410
sense 290.500
split 37.177
Range 35.410..37.177 at 4 nettime 396.667 catches 35.410..36.303
sense 396.667
split 36.303
Range 36.303..37.177 at 5 nettime 485.833 catches 36.303..37.050
sense 485.833
split 37.050
Range 37.050..37.177 at 6 nettime 573.000
Range 37.177..43.028 at 4 nettime 377.333 catches 37.177..38.163
sense 356.000
split 40.449
Range 38.163..40.449 at 5 nettime 461.667 catches 38.163..38.989
sense 453.333
split 39.706
Range 38.989..39.706 at 6 nettime 544.000
Range 39.706..40.449 at 6 nettime 534.000
Range 40.449..43.028 at 5 nettime 435.000 catches 40.449..41.379
sense 426.667
split 42.188
Range 41.379..42.188 at 6 nettime 512.000
Range 42.188..43.028 at 6 nettime 502.000
Range 43.028..66.667 at 3 nettime 241.000 catches 43.028..44.813
sense 201.500
split 53.598

Range 44.813..53.598 at 4 nettime 311.333 catches 44.813..46.253 sense 290.000

split 49.655

Range 46.253..49.655 at 5 nettime 379.167 catches 46.253..47.473 sense 370.833

split 48.539

Range 47.473..48.539 at 6 nettime 445.000

Range 48.539..49.655 at 6 nettime 435.000

Range 49.655..53.598 at 5 nettime 352.500 catches 49.655..51.064 sense 344.167

split 52.300

Range 51.064..52.300 at 6 nettime 413.000

Range 52.300..53.598 at 6 nettime 403.000

Range 53.598..66.667 at 4 nettime 258.667 catches 53.598..55.670 sense 237.333

split 60.674

Range 55.670..60.674 at 5 nettime 313.333 catches 55.670..57.447 sense 305.000

split 59.016

Range 57.447..59.016 at 6 nettime 366.000

Range 59.016..60.674 at 6 nettime 356.000

Range 60.674..66.667 at 5 nettime 286.667 catches 60.674..62.791 sense 278.333

split 64.671

Range 62.791..64.671 at 6 nettime 334.000

Range 64.671..66.667 at 6 nettime 324.000

Range 66.667..360.000 at 2 nettime 98.000 catches 66.667..73.469 sense 55.000

split 130.909

Range 73.469..130.909 at 3 nettime 137.000 catches 73.469..78.832 sense 122.000 split 88.525

Range 78.832..88.525 at 4 nettime 172.667 catches 78.832..83.398 sense 172.667

split 83.398

Range 83.398..88.525 at 5 nettime 205.833 catches 83.398..87.449
sense 205.833
split 87.449

Range 87.449..88.525 at 6 nettime 237.000
Range 88.525..130.909 at 4 nettime 152.667 catches 88.525..94.323
sense
131.333 split 109.645

Range 94.323..109.645 at 5 nettime 180.833 catches 94.323..99.539
sense
172.500 split 104.348

Range 99.539..104.348 at 6 nettime 207.000
Range 104.348..109.645 at 6 nettime 197.000
Range 109.645..130.909 at 5 nettime 154.167 catches 109.645..116.757
sense
145.833 split 123.429

Range 116.757..123.429 at 6 nettime 175.000
Range 123.429..130.909 at 6 nettime 165.000
Range 130.909..360.000 at 3 nettime 72.500 catches 130.909..148.966
sense
56.000 split 192.857

Range 148.966..192.857 at 4 nettime 86.667 catches 148.966..166.154
sense
86.667 split 166.154

Range 166.154..192.857 at 5 nettime 98.333 catches 166.154..183.051
sense
98.333 split 183.051

Range 183.051..192.857 at 6 nettime 108.000
Range 192.857..360.000 at 4 nettime 64.667 catches 192.857..222.680
sense
57.333 split 251.163

Range 222.680..251.163 at 5 nettime 70.833
Range 251.163..360.000 at 5 nettime 61.667 catches 251.163..291.892
sense
58.333 split 308.571

Range 291.892..308.571 at 6 nettime 64.000
Range 308.571..360.000 at 6 nettime 60.000

This puzzle is a riff on a suggestion made by Peter Carpenter during a drive through Wales.

As WITH MANY number tricks, you can understand this using simple algebra. The following should be within reach of a 14-year-old.

Suppose you are multiplying Y by Z. For Y, the number of fingers up is $Y - 5$. For example, if Y is 9, then 4 fingers are up. The number of fingers down is $10 - Y$ (1 when $Y = 9$).

1. We add up the up fingers and use that result for the 10s place:
   $(10(Y - 5)) + (10(Z - 5)) = 10Y - 50 + 10Z - 50 = 10Y + 10Z - 100$
2. We multiply the down fingers:
   $(10 - Y)(10 - Z) = 100 - 10Y - 10Z + YZ.$

When we add the two together, we get $10Y + 10Z - 100 + 100 - 10Y - 10Z + YZ$. All terms cancel except YZ. So the method gives us the product of Y and Z.

1. Mr. Red must wear blue pants, because Mr. Green wears green pants and Mr. Red already wears something red. So Mr. Blue wears red pants. Similarly, Mr. Green must wear a blue shirt, so Mr. Blue wears a green shirt. Mr. Green therefore wears a red hat, Mr. Red wears a green hat, and Mr. Blue wears a blue hat.

2. From (iii) and (iv), Mr. Red must wear a red hat. By (ii), therefore, Mr. Green wears a green hat and Mr. Blue wears a blue hat. By (i) and the above, Mr. Green wears a blue shirt. So, Mr. Red wears a green shirt and Mr. Blue wears a red shirt. Therefore, Mr. Blue wears green pants, a red shirt, and a blue hat.

Dinner Shakes

1. At any given table, no two people could be a couple. Therefore, the spouse of someone at the table must be at another table. So the stranger could shake hands with people at three tables for a total of 12 people.

2. If there were one big table, then 13 would be enough: an adjacent man/woman/man cannot include any couples.

1. The key observation is that the rightmost cycle and the upper-leftmost cycle each have a single lotus that connects them to the rest of the graph. Therefore Jamilla should start at one of those cycles and end at the other

	20					
21		19				
	22	18				
			17	5	4	
		16	6			3
	15	7	1	2		
		14	8			
		13	9			
	12	10				
		11				

2. The above explanation showed that one can start at either the upper-leftmost or -rightmost cycle and end at the other cycle. For each starting cycle, there are two starting points (on either side of the single connecting lotus), and for each cycle there are two ending points. So, starting at the upper-leftmost cycle yields four possibilities, and starting at the rightmost cycle yields four more. For each of these, there are two ways to go around the bottom cycle, so there are at least 16 possibilities altogether.

The Roads of Iguaçú

1. Cloe and Eli think it is not possible.

2. Eli said that it would cost $2 million and that GH and GI have to be two-way, as in

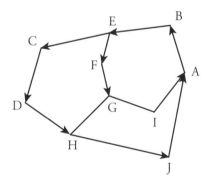

The roads without the arrowheads are two-way. Eli explains the reasoning this way: "It is possible to get from any outside node to another along the circular path, so that is six roads. The same goes for the interior loop. It remains to show that the two-way journeys between nodes C, D, H, and J and nodes F, G, and I can be done that fast.

Consider C first. C can go through H to I in four. C can get to F by going on the outside to E and then to F for a cost of seven. F can get to C in six. D can go to H, then G and I, or can go via J to F, all in six. F to D requires seven. H can go to F through J in five and to G and I in one and two. F, G, and I can reach H in two or less. J can reach all of these in six (for I). They can reach J by going through H in at most three."

3. Cloe explains: "Eli's solution to the last problem shows the way, because it ensures that C to F and F to D require less than six. Let's make two more roads two-way

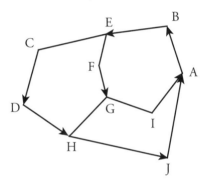

The Cowboy's Buckets

1. How to get 3 liters from a 7-liter container and a 12-liter container?

  i) Fill the 12-liter container.

  ii) Pour the 12 liters into the 7-liter container until the 7-liter container fills, leaving 5 liters in the 12-liter container.

  iii) Empty the 7-liter container.

  iv) Pour 5 liters from the 12-liter container into the 7-liter container.

  v) Fill the 12-liter container.

  vi) Pour into the 7-liter container until it fills, leaving 10 liters in the 12-liter container.

  vii) Empty the 7-liter container.

viii) Pour from the 12-liter container into the 7-liter container, leaving 3 liters in the 12-liter container.

2. How to get 2 liters from a bucket of unknown size, a 7-liter container, and a 12-liter container?

  i) Fill the 7-liter container.

  ii) Pour the 7 liters into the 12-liter container.

iii) Fill the 7-liter container.

iv) Pour the 7 liters into the 12-liter container until it fills. There are 2 liters left in the 7-liter container.

3. Hideki Yamasaki proposed the following method for measuring out just 1 liter. In the following, the first component represents the amount of liquid in the 12-liter container and the second the amount of liquid in the 7-liter container:

[0,0] [0,7] [7,0] [7,7] [12,2] [0,2] [2,0] [2,7] [9,0] [9,7] [12,4] [0,4] [4,0] [4,7] [11,0] [11,7] [12,6] [0,6] [6,0] [6,7] [12,1]

4. It's no longer possible to obtain 1 liter. In fact, the result of every pouring is either a multiple of 3 or 0.

SOLUTION TO
Lying Socks

1. Cloe started speaking almost immediately. "Ask two people whether the object is large or small. If they agree, then you trust them. If they don't, then one is a liar, so the third person must tell the truth. Ask the third person about the size, color, and object type. This gives you a total of five questions: three for the size and two for color and object. If they agree on the size, the color, and the type of object, you are done with six questions. If they agree on the size and color but differ about type, then ask the remaining person. The majority is honest. This gives seven questions.

2. Call the people A, B, C, D, E, and F. Ask A, B, and C about size. If there is no disagreement, then ask D, E, and F about color. If there is no disagreement about color, then ask any five about the type of object (sock or shoe). This scenario with its 11 questions turns out to be the worst of all, even though it may be that nobody ever lied. When liars show up early on, fewer questions are needed. Since there are quite a few cases, consider the decision tree

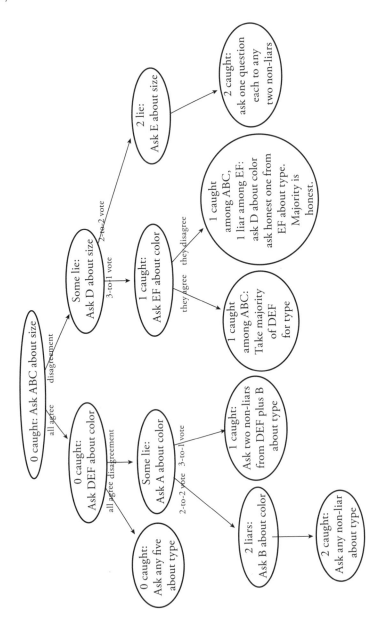

Start at the leftmost node (the root) and follow each outcome as you go right through the tree.

When Did the Last Train Leave?

FOR ALL THREE trains to cross a single bridge, the 1 P.M. train must be slow, the 3 P.M. train must be medium, and the last train must be fast. The 3 P.M. train will catch the 1 P.M. train at 5 P.M. So that's when the crash must have occurred. At that point, both trains would have traveled 400 kilometers. The fast train therefore traveled 400 kilometers by 5 P.M. The fast train goes that far in $\frac{4}{3}$ hours or 1 hour and 20 minutes. Therefore, the last fast train left at 3:40 P.M.

1. "Yes," Eli answered. "You take one assistant with you to a door and send the other assistant to another door. If the assistant with you tells the truth as you see it and you don't find the diamond, then do the opposite of what the other assistant says. If the assistant with you lies and you don't find the diamond, then do exactly what the other assistant says."

2. Eli suggests the following: "Bring two with you to a door. If they both lie, then the other is a truth-teller. If they both tell the truth, then the other is an unconditional liar. So do the opposite of what he or she says. If the two disagree, then the conditional liar is the third assistant and he will tell the truth."

SOLUTION TO
Papyrus Math

1. The total area of the two smaller squares still equals 100, so $x^2 + (\frac{3}{4}x)^2 = 100$. Therefore $\frac{25}{16}x^2 = 100$. Multiplying both sides by $\frac{16}{25}$, we get $x^2 = 64$. So, $x = 8$ and the smaller parcel has a side length of 6.

2. The total is $5F - 10d = 115$. Therefore, dividing by 5, we get $F - 2d = 23$. We know that $F - 4d$, the inheritance of the youngest, is a whole number between 10 and 20. So, d cannot be 1, because that would make $F = 25$ and $F - 4d = 21$. Nor can d be 7, because then $F - 4d$ would be $23 - 14 = 9$. Therefore $d = 6$ and the quantities of coins for each child in descending order are: 35, 29, 23, 17, and 11.

Bodyguards for an Ancient Tyrant

1. From the warm-up, we know that C and E must be loyal and so must one of A and D. Therefore C, A, and D are solid for the first 8 hours, then C, E for the next 8 hours, and then E, A, D for the last 8 hours of each day.

2. Here are the accusation links symbolically: (A,B), (B,C), (C,D), (D,E), (E,F), (F,G), (B,E), (G,D), (F,C).

A hitting set is a set of nodes S such that every accusation shares at least one node with S. The three nodes B, D, and F constitute a minimal hitting set. Any larger one would imply that a majority of the guards were disloyal, and we know that is not the case.

Therefore, all the others are good. One of many possible schedules would therefore be A and C for the first 8 hours, E and G for the next 8, and then back to A and C.

Election Fraud in Verity

1. There can be at most three pollsters meeting these conditions. Here is why. Each pollster must miss 13 Wendy voters (because there are 51 in total, but only 38 seen by each pollster). No two pollsters miss the same Wendy voter, because every pair of pollsters interviews all 100 voters. If we number the Wendy voters W1 to W51, then we can imagine that pollster A misses W1 to W13, pollster B misses W14 to W26, and pollster C misses W27 to W39. There are not enough more Wendy voters for a fourth pollster to miss, so there can be only three pollsters.

2. Number the Fred voters F1 to F49. Pollster A could interview W14 to W51 and F1 to F42. Then pollster B could interview W1 to W13 and W27 to W51 as well as F8 to F49. Finally, pollster C could interview W1 to W16 and W40 to W51, as well as F1 to F7 and F15 to F49.

3. As the solution to the first question showed, this result would not be possible with five honest pollsters. So Fred was right: Wendy stole the election.

Tom Rokicki helped enormously with these solutions.

Treasure Arrow

LET'S FIRST SOLVE the problem symbolically. The pole has length L and mass Mp and the arrowhead has weight Ma. We represent the pole's mass Mp as a point mass at the center.

Now let's say we have five elastics, including ones at the ends and at every quarter point.

We know that the lengths of the bands must form a straight line, because the pole is stiff. This observation (made by my colleague Alan Siegel) gives us a constraint in addition to balanced torque and balanced vertical force. Here, $s1$ is the stretch of the leftmost band in centimeters. Delta is the difference from one band to the next to the right, again in centimeters.

$$s1 + \Delta = s2$$
$$s2 + \Delta = s3$$
$$s3 + \Delta = s4$$
$$s4 + \Delta = s5$$

The balance of vertical forces gives us:

$$5 \times s1 + (1 + 2 + 3 + 4)\Delta = Mp + Ma$$

The balance of torques gives us:

$$L \times \frac{Mp}{2} \text{ from the pole}$$

Countertorques:

$$L \times (s1 + \frac{3}{4} \times (s1 + \Delta) + (\frac{1}{2}) \times (s1 + 2\Delta) + (\frac{1}{4})(s1 + 3\Delta))$$
$$= L \times ((s1 \times (1 + \frac{3}{4} + \frac{1}{2} + \frac{1}{4})) + \Delta \times (\frac{3}{4} + 1 + \frac{3}{4}))$$
$$= L \times (2.5\, s1 + 2.5\Delta)$$
$$= 2.5\, L\, (s1 + \Delta)$$

So (1) $\frac{Mp}{2} = 2.5\,(s1 + \Delta)$, from torque balance

(2) $Mp + Ma = 5\,(s1 + 2\Delta)$, from vertical balance

From (2), $\frac{Mp + Ma}{5} - 2\Delta = s1.$

Therefore, using the torque balance,

$$\frac{Mp}{2} = 2.5(s1 + \Delta)$$
$$= 2.5(\frac{Mp + Ma}{5} - 2\Delta + \Delta)$$
$$= 2.5(\frac{Mp + Ma}{5} - \Delta)$$
$$= 2.5\frac{Mp + Ma}{5} - 2.5\Delta$$
$$= \frac{Mp + Ma}{2} - 2.5\Delta$$

So, $2.5\Delta = \frac{Ma}{2}$ and $\Delta = \frac{Ma}{5}$

Therefore, $s1 = \frac{Mp}{5} + \frac{Ma}{5} - 2\frac{Ma}{5} = \frac{Mp}{5} - \frac{Ma}{5}.$

This implies that if $Mp = Ma$, then $s1 = 0$. Since these two quantities are equal, $s1$ must equal 0 so the left band is at its rest length of 1 meter and the right band is down 60 centimeters so the arrow is pointing to a point that is 100 cm + 2 × 60 cm = 2.2 meters from the top, approximately. Further, Δ is 15 centimeters ($\frac{60}{4}$). So, $Mp = Ma = 75$ kilograms.

As Carl Smotricz of Frankfurt points out, the 2.2 meters is not quite right. He notes that because the arrow is not quite horizontal, the horizontal distance between the two ends of the arrow is less than 10 meters. In fact it is $\sqrt{10^2 - 0.6^2} = 9.98$. So the arrowhead has dipped 0.6 meters for each 9.98 meters of horizontal distance. Extending this line to the wall (Carl used trigonometry, but let's do this in a more elementary way), there would be a further dip of some amount x for the next 10 meters of horizontal distance. So, $x = 0.6 \times \frac{10}{9.98}$. This gives an extra 0.601 meters. So the arrow in fact points to 2.201 meters below the ceiling.

Decryption of letter from Rose to Ecco (though addressed to Baskerhound):

Dear Dr. Baskerhound,

My climbing partner Scot was giving me a ride from Bend to Goldendale. As we crossed the Hood River Bridge, the pick-up in front of us stopped and the one behind us pinned us to one place. Two beefy thugs jumped out of each truck jumped out and started towards our car. "Get the apostate," said one of them. All four of them wore white shirts having a large cross rising from fire in red, all in red.

I knew who they meant. "Don't worry about me," I told Scot. "As soon as I get out, take off." I opened the door, climbed the guard rail, and jumped off the bridge, leaving my wallet under the railing. (As I hoped, the police found it and the papers picked up the fact that I was missing. I wanted to do this without involving Scot.) Luckily the beefboys didn't see it. When I hit the water, I blacked out momentarily. When I came to, I saw that Scot had weaved away. I saw muzzle flashes too. So I swam under water and got out of there. I can't tell you where I'm hiding but know that I'm recovering quickly. Be sure to stay in hiding yourself.

Now I need to figure out a way to convey the ballots to the _Oregonian_, the newspaper of record out here. If you forward this to Professor Scarlet and Dr. Ecco, maybe they can advise me through the Bleecker Street beggar. Tell them to use a similar code.

Warm Regards,
Rose
P.S. Mom and the twins are safe and far away.

Warriors of the Rapture

1. There are 34 possibilities for an eight-rung ladder. The sequence of numbers of possibilities is 2 3 5 8 13 21 34. Let's consider the case of six rungs. The first move can be either to rung 1 or rung 2. If rung 1, there are 8 possible paths to climb the remaining five rungs using the solution for five rungs computed in the warm-up. If rung 2, there are 5 possible paths for the remaining four rungs so 13 (8 + 5) altogether.

2. It is best to start with 1 step (no skips). If that is correct, then you won't be corrected and there will be 21 paths from rung 1. If it is incorrect, then there will be 13 more paths from rung 2. So, at most, you will try 21 paths.

Decryption of Ecco's letter to Rose and Baskerhound:

```
To: R and B
From: Ecco


My friends, beware the Truth Mirage. The
last election introduced a new tactic.
Suppose your candidate has an embarrassing
```

past. You fabricate a piece of evidence
exposing that past in the most graphic
terms. You let your opponents publi-
cize it.

When that single piece of evidence turns
out to be a forgery—turns out to be a
Truth Mirage—all allegations of wrongdoing
on the topic are discredited.

If the mounting evidence of skullduggery
surrounding the election in Ohio is to be
believed, we must be sure that what Rose
has in her hands is not another Truth
Mirage. The best way to fight one Truth
Mirage is with another. Oh, and humor
makes for a good story.

E

1. Jeanne Boyarsky and Michael Birken both proposed excellent solutions. Jeanne showed that 36 could be computed with three 4s: $4 \times \frac{4}{.4R}$. Birken showed that all but two of the numbers up to 40 could be done with just three 4s. This included such remarkable insights as that 37 can be rendered as:

$$\frac{4! + \sqrt{.4R}}{\sqrt{.4R}} = \frac{74}{3} \times \frac{3}{2}.$$

Scott Kassan noticed that 36 could be rendered as $\frac{4!}{\sqrt{.4R}}$. $4 \times 3 \times 2 \times 1 = 24$ and $\sqrt{.4R} = \frac{2}{3}$.

$0 = 4 - 4$

$1 = \frac{4}{4}$

$2 = \sqrt{4}$

$3 = 4 - \frac{4}{4}$

$4 = 4$

$5 = 4 + \frac{4}{4}$

$$6 = \frac{4!}{4}$$

$$7 = \frac{4 + 4!}{4}$$

$$8 = 4 + 4$$

$$9 = \frac{4}{.4R}$$

$$10 = \frac{4}{.4}$$

$$11 = \frac{44}{4}$$

$$12 = (4 \times 4) - 4$$

$$13 = \frac{4}{.4R} + 4$$

$$14 = 4 + \frac{4}{.4}$$

$$15 = \frac{4!}{4 \times .4}$$

$$16 = 4 \times 4$$

$$17 = \text{(requires four 4s)} \ (4 \times 4) + \frac{4}{4}$$

$$18 = \frac{4 + 4}{.4R}$$

$$19 = 4! - \frac{\sqrt{4}}{.4}$$

$$20 = 4! - 4$$

$$21 = 4! - \sqrt{\frac{4}{.4R}}$$

$$22 = \frac{44}{\sqrt{4}}$$

$$23 = 4! - \frac{4}{4}$$

$$24 = 4!$$

$$25 = \frac{4}{.4 \times .4}$$

$$26 = \sqrt{4} + 4!$$

$$27 = \frac{4!}{.4R + .4R}$$

$$28 = 4 + 4!$$

$29 = \frac{\sqrt{4}}{.4} + 4!$

$30 = \frac{4!}{.4 + .4}$

$31 = $ (requires four 4s) $4! + \frac{4! + 4}{4}$

$32 = (4 + 4) \times 4$

$33 = 4! + \frac{4}{.4R}$

$34 = \frac{4}{.4} + 4!$

$35 = \frac{4! - \sqrt{.4R}}{\sqrt{.4R}}$

$36 = \frac{4}{.4R} \times 4$

$37 = \frac{4! + \sqrt{.4R}}{\sqrt{.4R}}$

$38 = \sqrt{4} + \frac{4!}{\sqrt{.4R}}$

$39 = \frac{\sqrt{4} + 4!}{\sqrt{.4R}}$

$40 = 44 - 4$

2. Beyond 40, Birken was able to capture all the numbers up to 112.

$41 = \frac{.4 + (4 \times 4)}{.4}$

$42 = 44 - \sqrt{4}$

$43 = 44 - \frac{4}{4}$

$44 = 44$

$45 = 44 + \frac{4}{4}$

$46 = 44 + \sqrt{4}$

$47 = 44 + \sqrt{\frac{4}{.4R}}$

$48 = 4 + 44$

$$49 = 44 + \frac{\sqrt{4}}{.4}$$

$$50 = 44 + \frac{4!}{4}$$

$$51 = \frac{(4! + .4) - 4}{.4}$$

$$52 = 4 + 4 + 44$$

$$53 = \frac{4}{.4R} + 44$$

$$54 = \frac{4!}{.4R}$$

$$55 = \frac{44}{.4 + .4}$$

$$56 = \frac{4!}{.4} - 4$$

$$57 = \frac{4! + .4}{.4} - 4$$

$$58 = 4 + \frac{4!}{.4R}$$

$$59 = \frac{4! - .4}{.4}$$

$$60 = \frac{4!}{.4}$$

$$61 = \frac{.4 + 4!}{.4}$$

$$62 = \frac{44}{\sqrt{.4R}} - 4$$

$$63 = \frac{4 + 4!}{.4R}$$

$$64 = \frac{4^4}{4}$$

$$65 = \frac{4 + 4^4}{4}$$

$$66 = \frac{44}{\sqrt{.4R}}$$

$$67 = \frac{4 + 4!}{.4R} + 4$$

$$68 = 44 + 4!$$

$$69 = \frac{4 - .4 + 4!}{.4}$$

$$70 = \frac{4! + 4}{.4}$$

$$71 = \frac{4 + .4 + 4!}{.4}$$

$$72 = 44 + 4! + 4$$

$$73 = \sqrt{\sqrt{\sqrt{4^{4!}}}} + \frac{4}{.4R}$$

$$74 = 4 + \frac{4! + 4}{.4}$$

$$75 = \frac{44}{.4R} - 4!$$

$$76 = (4 \times (4! - 4)) - 4$$

$$77 = \left(\frac{4}{.4R}\right)^{\sqrt{4}} - 4$$

$$78 = \frac{4!}{.4R} + 4!$$

$$79 = \sqrt{\left(\frac{4}{.4R}\right)^4} - \sqrt{4}$$

$$80 = 4 \times (4! - 4)$$

$$81 = \left(\frac{4}{4} - 4\right)^4$$

$$82 = (4 + 4!) + \frac{4!}{.4R}$$

$$83 = 4! - \frac{.4 - 4!}{.4}$$

$$84 = 4! + \frac{4!}{.4}$$

$$85 = \frac{4! + \frac{4}{.4}}{.4}$$

$$86 = \frac{44}{.4} - 4!$$

$$87 = (4 \times 4!) - \frac{4}{.4R}$$

$$88 = 44 + 44$$

$$89 = \frac{\frac{4!}{\sqrt{.4R}} - .4}{.4}$$

$$90 = \frac{4}{.4R - .4}$$

$$91 = \frac{.4 + \frac{4!}{\sqrt{.4R}}}{.4}$$

$$92 = (4 \times 4!) - 4$$

$$93 = (4 \times 4!) - \sqrt{\frac{4}{.4R}}$$

$$94 = 4 + \frac{4}{.4R - .4}$$

$$95 = \frac{44}{.4R} - 4$$

$$96 = 4! \times 4$$

$$97 = \frac{44}{.4R} - \sqrt{4}$$

$$98 = \frac{44 - .4R}{.4R}$$

$$99 = \frac{44}{.4R}$$

$$100 = \frac{44 - 4}{.4}$$

$$101 = \frac{44}{.4R} + \sqrt{4}$$

$$102 = (4^4 \times .4) - .4$$

$$103 = \frac{44}{.4R} + 4$$

$$104 = 44 + \frac{4!}{.4}$$

$$105 = \frac{44 - \sqrt{4}}{.4}$$

$$106 = \frac{44}{.4} - 4$$

$$107 = \frac{4! + (4! - .4R)}{.4R}$$

$$108 = \frac{4 + 44}{.4R}$$

$$109 = \frac{44 - .4}{.4}$$

$$110 = \frac{44}{.4}$$

$$111 = \frac{444}{4}$$

$$112 = 4 \times (4 + 4!)$$

Notes on a method of solution: to start with, it helps to learn a technique called dynamic programming. The idea is to use solutions to simpler problems when solving more complex ones. So, when finding a solution to, say, 68, one can look at all pairs that add up to 68, for example 67 and 1, 66 and 2, and so on, to see whether combining those solutions might be helpful. In the event, the solutions for 44 and 24 worked out, thus $68 = 44 + (4!)$. Multiplication by numbers greater than 1 works the same way. Division and subtraction are more tricky. One idea is to skip values that can't be produced by combining smaller numbers and then revisit them after filling in larger numbers. Thus simpler need not mean smaller.

Decryption of note from Baskerhound to Ecco:

> *Ecco, what do we do? How can we get a package to a well-known place?*

Decryption of Ecco's reply to Rose and Baskerhound:

```
R and B:

Approach from many sides and then one
more. As Baskerhound knows from the affair
of the diamond shipments, it takes long to
find reliable middlemen. You'll need a bet-
ter code.
```

Are There Spies?

1. Suppose again that A, D, and E think there is a spy. A says: "At least one of A and B thinks there is a spy." B says: "At least one of A and B thinks there is no spy." D and E each say: "At least two of C, D, and E think there is a spy." C says: "At least one of C, D, and E thinks there is no spy." This preserves Anonymity because A and B are treated symmetrically, as are C, D, and E. It satisfies Three Spy, because the two groups are disjoint. Two think "no spy" for the same reason.

2. To prove that exactly four people believe there is a spy, it is necessary for someone to say that one person in some group doesn't believe there is a spy. Because the group cannot contain more than three people, the remaining two people must think there is a spy. This violates our Anonymity condition.

3. To prove that at least four people believe there is a spy, while keeping all the conditions, have some people make more than one statement. The end result is that for every three people of the five, X, Y, Z, someone has claimed that two out of the three people in X, Y, Z say there is a spy. If three or fewer people thought there was a spy, this statement could not be made about some such triplet.

Tom Rokicki suggested the generalization that is still open.

1. If the first one is blue, then here are the remaining possibilities:

> Ba Bb
> Ba Rb
> Ba Ra
> Bb Ba
> Bb Ra
> Bb Rb

In 2 out of 6, we get two blues. So the probability of two blues given that the first is blue is $\frac{1}{3}$.

If we are told that at least one is blue, then we have the following 10 possibilities:

> Ra Ba
> Ra Bb
> Rb Ba
> Rb Bb
> Ba Bb
> Ba Rb

    Ba Ra
    Bb Ba
    Bb Ra
    Bb Rb

Only 2 of the 10 give us a pair of blue socks. So we have a $\frac{1}{5}$ chance of getting a matching pair.

2. For the five boxes, consider them laid out in a row. There are 10 possible arrangements where 1 means "has money" and 0 means "doesn't":

    11000
    10100
    10010
    10001
    01100
    01010
    01001
    00110
    00101
    00011

Without loss of generality, suppose you pick the first box. You have a 4 in 10 chance of winning. Now, suppose that your adversary opens two other boxes that have zeros. These are marked with xs below. This leaves:

    11xx0
    1x1x0
    1xx10
    1xx01
    011xx
    01x1x
    01xx1

0xllx
0xlxl
0xxll

where two of the 0s in each row are now xs. If you happened to choose
one of the good boxes in your first guess, then switching gives you
a probability of $\frac{1}{2}$ of landing on the other. If your first guess wasn't
good, then switching will surely give you a good result. Thus switching
gives a good result in $\frac{1}{2} \times \frac{4}{10} + \frac{6}{10} = \frac{8}{10}$ of the cases. If you don't
switch, you still win in $\frac{4}{10}$ of the cases. Switching improves your
likelihood of winning by a factor of 2!

By the way, you might have thought of another visualization consisting of a circle having two 1s (representing the $10,000 boxes) and
three 0s (representing the moneyless boxes).

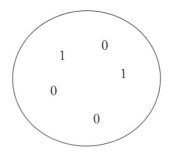

Picking a box corresponds to drawing an arrow to one of the
numbers. Two out of five times this will be to a 1.

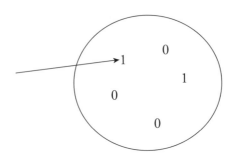

Now cross out two 0s, leaving the 1 you were pointing to, a second 1, and a 0.

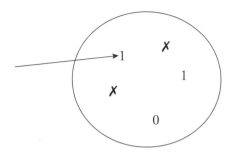

So switching gives a probability of $\frac{1}{2}$ of winning. Similarly, if you first point to a 0, then eliminating two 0s leaves only a 1 if you switch.

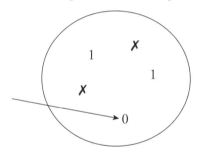

3. If your adversary opens only one moneyless box, then here is how the probabilities change. If you had picked a winner at first, your chance of winning with a switch would be $\frac{1}{3}$ (thus, $\frac{2}{5} \times \frac{1}{3}$, altogether). If you had picked a loser at first, your chance of winning with a switch is $\frac{2}{3}$ (thus, $\frac{3}{5} \times \frac{2}{3}$ altogether). Adding these up gives $\frac{8}{15}$. By contrast, sticking with your original choice still gives you a $\frac{2}{5}$ chance of winning.

4. If you know that at least one child is a girl, then the probability that both are girls is just $\frac{1}{3}$. This is just like the dime and penny setup. There are four equally likely family types (B represents boy and G represents girl):

BB
BG
GB
GG

The first one is impossible and two out of the other three have only one girl. On the other hand, if you see a girl playing outside, then the probability that both are girls is $\frac{1}{2}$, as pointed out by Charles A. Castleman. Why the difference? Intuitively, because a two-girl family is more likely to have a girl playing outside. But here is the analysis. Again there are four family types: BB, BG, GB, and GG. In addition, either the older or the younger is outside, so represent the sex of the child outside as the third letter. Thus, BGG represents a family that has an older boy, a younger girl, and the girl that is playing outside. Since any kid is equally likely to be playing outside, the following are all equally likely:

BBB — for the older boy
BBB
BGB
BGG
GBG
GBB
GGG — for the older girl
GGG

If we see a girl playing outside, we can be in one of these situations:

BGG
GBG
GGG — for the older girl
GGG

Half the time the other sibling is a girl.

Further reading: The boxes-with-money puzzle is a variant on a puzzle posed by Marilyn vos Savant in 1990 called the Monty Hall puzzle. In that puzzle, there were three doors, only one of which concealed a treasure. The contestant would point to a door without opening it, Monty Hall would then always open a treasure-less door, and the contestant would be asked to decide whether to switch or not. Marilyn correctly asserted that the contestant should switch. She received a number of letters from professors who disagreed, sometimes vehemently, but then later had to retract their objections. My motivation for presenting this puzzle in a more complex setting is to show that such puzzles are easy when viewed properly. The puzzle has an even longer history, having been posed by my eminent predecessor Martin Gardner and by Joseph Bertrand in the nineteenth century. See http://www.barryispuzzled.com/zmonty.htm to learn more about the history of the problem.

Fair Counts

HERE IS ECCO'S solution:

When I as a voter leave the voting booth, I remove the backing paper, which has the ballot number on it as well. If a recount ever occurs, I can check that my ballot was included by seeing whether a ballot having my scribbling field was present. Another ballot having the same number but with something different in the scribbling field would indicate fraud. The absence of a ballot with my ballot number would also indicate fraud.

Some people would rather not keep information that could be tied back to their votes. Such people can discard the backing copy.

Photocopying the scribbling field of the ballot and then selecting different candidates is possible, but then the impressions done on the backing paper would not be consistent with those on the ballot.

The only part of the ballot available for verification by the public (as opposed to the trusted recounters) would be the scribble field. This would prevent vote selling, since nobody among the general public could see any ballot.

Finally, the assumption about not being able to write on the backing paper ensures the physical integrity of the backing paper even weeks after the election is over. This would prevent fraudulent complaints. Such functionality could be achieved by a photographic process in which exposure to light or air changes the surface of the paper. Alternatively, the ripping off of the backing paper would be done by machine, which could add a coating to the backing paper before dropping the ballot into a box.